FIC
RYC

MAR 3 0 2010

Black Table

ALSO BY RYCJ

GEM
LEIATRA'S RHAPSODY
PRETTY INSIDE OUT
SOMETHING XTRA WILD

COMING SOON

TEHUELCHE

BLACK TABLE

RYCJsBookPage
Pennsylvania

For details regarding bulk purchases about this book and others write: Rhonda Y.C. Johnson, 1057 P.O. Box Bryn Mawr, Pennsylvania, 19010-7057

OSAAT Entertainment, 1057 P.O. Box
Bryn Mawr, Pennsylvania, 19010-7057

All rights reserved. No part of this book may be reproduced or transmitted in any form or by any means, graphic, electronic, or mechanical, including photocopying, recording, taping, or by any information storage retrieval system, without the written permission of the publisher.

First Edition.

Copyright © 2007 RYCJ, Black table. Memoir/Essays.

Library of Congress Control Number: 2008908938

ISBN: 978-0-9818256-1-8

Published in the United States of America

"*Give a man a fish and he will eat for a day. Teach him how to fish and he will eat for a lifetime.*"

Chinese proverb

for my family

Bless This Table

So what influenced this book?

Three other books.

As it came to be, three books jumped on me, or maybe even me on them, at a time when I was zoned out. That being, I was out of a job and nearly out of my mind as I halfway expected would be the case when I left my career to reorganize my priorities.

In my down time, and I do mean down time in any which way the phrase can be construed, I got to reading books I thought might pick up my speed. Yes, at speeds probably in excess of sound, I had run clean out of my mind. Nevertheless, do not think that in any way meant I wanted to slow down. What I needed to do was find my mind. And the sooner the better.

The irony however was, all in the paradox the three books I chose to read in spectacular succession related to my sequence of thoughts at the moment I came across them.

Okay, so here goes it, omitting titles in order to be honest without offending anyone.

In my slightly depressed state... well wait, let me rephrase that. In my quite paranoid state I thought traveling halfway across the country would help soothe my thoughts running back and forth from nightmare to nightmare. I even took this trip by train, since going by plane I just knew would increase my paranoia. I mean, I really thought this going halfway across the country by train was a very good decision. And so, what is a good way to travel halfway across country by train?

You've got it. Traveling with a good book.

Boggled down with an awkward agglomeration of luggage I ran out the door with a celebrated book I hadn't yet read but had gone out of my way to have autographed. I was just so sure this book was going to add comfort to my trip. I really thought I knew this author. Two or three of her other books gave me the greatest kick. I really, literally, had no idea, even though I must admit, I toted along two of my own books in case this read turned out to be not how I preferred to celebrate.

I didn't get a chance to pull out my autographed celebrated jewel on the first leg of my journey because I met a passenger who held my attention with an interesting dialogue for more than three quarters of that leg of the trip. In fact, I also need to credit him for inspiring my book as well. He turned out to be a well-read man who summarized a number of other seemingly interesting books I never heard of. But oh well, we ended up parting company at the first train station. He went one way, and I the other.

On the train during the wee hours of the night, after my nerves had settled to some restless degree, I again thought about the jewel I had brought along for comfort. I slipped the book out of my bag and ran my hand over the smooth beveled art on the cover.

It was a pretty book. Raised gold star against a seawater blue backdrop wearing a cool pair of shades, I couldn't imagine anything less than being privy to warm sentimental secrets that would pick me up. I patted the cover sighing to no one in particular, "Baby hold on, you just wait…"

But then sleep found me long before I could get to the part of actually opening the book. Maybe it was the swaying motion of the train and its soft hum that rocked me so quickly to sleep.

I'm not sure what stirred me next—my cell phone ringing, the man seated beside me fidgeting in his sleep fighting to keep warm, or dreaming about the beautiful book still clutched in my arms. Whichever it was, I awoke in the wee hours of the morning.

Being warm and partially comfortable made me feel

for the man seated beside me. I removed the blanket wrapped around my face and placed it over the quivering man. Quietly he thanked me and went back to sleep.

Suddenly I was wide-eyed awake. I looked through the darkness, taking note of a young man seated across the aisle. He had finally turned off his laptop and was nestled in a deep sleep. I wanted to wake him and ask him to charge my laptop battery, but he looked too comfortable to stir. Besides, I had already bugged him earlier to charge my cell phone.

I hoisted myself up a bit to see if everyone was that sound asleep. They were. Heads tilted back, leaning sideways, and covers pulled up to many necks was an understated solace indescribable. It made it the perfect time to make my way to the observation car ahead to read my jewel.

There was only one other person in the observation car. A woman who I took for being a passenger like myself was sitting at one of the dining tables looking like she was waiting for a meal. But when she saw me, she balked about being thirsty. The train was all out of water, which I didn't even think to hand over my last bottle of water. The train ride experience being just what I needed had me too darn psyched.

The big empty car with its long inviting windows breezing through the night made me feel privileged. I had all that visual to myself. Hidden dams and bridges and seemingly untouched naked farms basking beneath an almost onyx sky wasn't meant for me to see, not when most I knew were busy brewing coffee preparing for another workday. It was the best moment of the entire ride. I sat back and exhaled, and at last opened my autographed celebrated jewel.

Right then, and there, it started all over again.

Thank God the whole world hadn't opened that book. I really don't want to get into blaming anyone for my downward plight, but beginning with opening my autographed jewel also marked the beginning of my return to sinking back into a deep depression.

Long story short, after tying the introduction of this jewel in with its title, one thought led to the next. Before long, a thought that began with an open celebration of pain without relief, conveniently sped up to, "Oh my God! It's a holiday weekend. This train may not make it to my destination!"

I slapped the book closed and haven't opened it since. After transferring trains and douching my face with cold water in a portable bathroom, I became so wound up that I ran back to my seat, scrambled together my awkward collection of luggage, and jumped off the train.

Absolutely dreadful; just me and my awkward agglomeration of luggage toppled on a deserted platform. My panic attack left me stranded in Chicago. But thank God for my husband. I fuss about his pokiness all the time but had no complaints about his speed during my greatest time of need.

In one phone call he chauffeured me through a train station where I'd never been; ushered me to a taxi where a cab driver delivered me to a hotel near O'Hare's Airport. And the very next morning had me on my way to Philadelphia, which flying was the last way I wanted to travel. I'm not blaming my celebrated jewel, and then again I must be, but I haven't opened the book since.

Ironically, this brings me to the next book I picked up. A gluten for punishment, huh?

After a week in Philadelphia, incidentally, the last place I thought would settle my nerves, I came upon another book. Again, I am not blaming anyone for anything. It was just so ironic that out of the plethora of books in this large Barnes & Noble bookstore, that this particular title would catch my eye.

Instinctively I thought, "Oh, so here we go again. Someone else to tell me not to listen to the person who told me eggs weren't good for me."

I just knew I was going to open the book and learn if I started back eating eggs I would grow leaner longer legs, wiser eyes, and an extra brain. Yet, I really needed this laugh. I laughed even harder noting how the author, probably during the final phase of printing the remaining 30,000 copies of the book realized, "Umm, I forgot some assholes," and then added more insults to an oddly short list.

Bless This Table   XV

That too, however innocent, was a clever catch. I also have to admit I didn't even cheat. Without my glasses I glanced over the title, flipped the book over—couldn't see diddly—and then thumbed through the book long enough to make out two names I immediately recognized. This made me curious.

Why would someone think those two people were to blame for anything? I looked at the price, which thirteen bucks was not a whole lot to sacrifice, and purchased a copy remarking to the clerk who also thought the title was interesting, "Who knows, maybe I'm listed somewhere in here."

The clerk laughed, "Hey, I probably am too."

I ended up reading this book in its entirety. I really enjoyed the book, too. The author's loose lipped thoughts really made me think. It made me think, "Hey, who really is influencing my values… and subsequently the blame for my pucked up plight?"

This leads to the third book. The book that finally flipped my script.

On the return trip to Texas I stopped again in Chicago to change trains. It was a long layover. But ahead of time I planned how I was going to spend this down time. Not forgetting about a bar I spotted on the inbound leg, but was too delirious to pay a visit, I found a seat in a cozy corner and opened this book—the third book.

Thanks to the third book three hours flew by. I wanted to lick my fingers after I finished reading the book. Laughing from beginning to end, I couldn't get out of my head how I wanted to write like that.

...Well not exactly like that, but like that. I wanted to write a book where I could lighten some poor soul's load. After my frantic run through the Windy City, breezing back and forth here and there as if I had looked over the edge of Earth and saw my pucked up plight, I realized that some of us really do need a break from hardcore idealistic reality. This book is for all those who want to chill for a moment.

Let's Bless this Table...

(*L*eft) my brother, Ronnie, (*C*enter) me,
(*R*ight) my sister, Lisa.
1966

Entrées

CHAPTER ONE
AVENUE OF THE ARTS
1. Goshladang! 1
2. Saying Grace 5
3. Little Rusty Wallace 12

CHAPTER TWO
EINSTEIN'S COBBLESTONES
4. Whippin' Machine 18
5. The Incubator 24
6. Love on the Black Hand Side ... 32
7. Pink Floyd 38
8. No Place Like Home 43
9. Rhythm & Blues 51

CHAPTER THREE
RITTENHOUSE STREET
10. The Meaning of Christmas 61
11. Daddy Steppin' n Fletchin' 67
12. Gettin' the Bad Guy 72
13. The Big Blue Valley 77
14. Rosemary 88
15. Fat Cat 96
16. Jim Beam 103

CHAPTER FOUR
VENANGO HALL LEFTOVERS
17. Nobody's Food 111
18. Ros-Poke 121

CHAPTER FIVE
CENTER CITY ATTRACTIONS
19. The Black Man 127
20. Carole Brady 132
21. A Hooligan, A Painted Cat & Humpty
.... 136
22. Sue-Ellen 140
23. gooood Morning 144
24. Sunday 148

CHAPTER SIX
SOFT PRETZELS & CHEESESTEAKS
25. Der Reiters 153
26. Mr. Romance 161
27. Piggy Packin' Bears 168

CHAPTER SEVEN
LITTLE QUAKERS
28. Any Fool 188
29. Slip and Slide Scrap'ems 196
30. Two Peas in a Pod 202
31. The Boys 209

CHAPTER ONE

"Avenue of the Arts"

GOSHLADANG!

When I try going over how things really got started for us, I find myself wandering around the first apple tree in the world telling myself, like the one incident where the apple fell way far from the tree, I have to start somewhere. That's what everyone keeps telling me.

"You have to start somewhere."

But what people really mean is that I have to start from what I know. Well, when I think of the making and coming together of my parents, and ultimately the setting of our table, Goshladang instantly comes to mind. Goshladang is what the apple said when it fell way left of the tree.

So let's get this straight, right off the cuff. Goshladang is a male character that spends every waking second—so he never sleeps—matchmaking. Goshladang just sits around all day, and all night, selecting among other cumbersome activities he oversees, who goes with whom, and when, and for what cause. His matchmaking detail is his most important detail. It is an arduous detail he doesn't take on haphazardly, but one he enjoys the ten jubilees and one Yucca Mountain out of just the same. Goshladang takes real pride in his work.

I mean, matchmaking is one serious issue. Too many mixed-matches and the whole state of civilization is thrown into chaos. Goshladang doesn't want this. The first time this happened he snatched the whole apple tree from the ground and kicked each apple, one by one, out into a deadened black sea. After the fact he realized his mistake. There was no need for him to have gone to that extent. What he should have done is what he ended up doing. Starting from somewhere.

I can just picture Goshladang sitting on a great big sandy mound way up high just beyond the last zenith picking his toes and daydreaming about 'what if' and 'how about'. That's what it looked like he was doing when I first spotted him.

He was working on yet another project when for about the trillionth time he goes, "Ah, ha!"

Of course Goshladang thought he had it—again, which brings me to the making and setting of our black table.

"Umm," Goshladang must have hummed, "Let me see… ah yes, right there. I'll need this one… and umm," he was back to mulling around again, "… and umm, ah yeah… and that one."

Goshladang was sure of himself. He was satisfied with his pickings. Now I won't dare go into which one of my parents was the 'this one' and the 'that one'. It's so not the point. The only point here is that Goshladang was satisfied with this particular project.

The many sleepless hours he spent expanding and combing and measuring and merging his work went far beyond personality likes and dislikes. Goshladang had to look at important matters such as physics and chemistry. He had to separate criteria's such as history and geography, and then he needed to swish all these factors around the original image of mankind like mouthwash, crossing his fingers and hoping for the best. It was a complicated and arduous detail that required knowing a thing or two about balance.

I know this all sounds silly. But what I am saying here is our black table hardly came by way of coincidence. Somebody up there had stewed over and mulled over this table long, long before lacquer was even black. I mean, what's lacquer anyway? Oh, Please! Goshladang stained the resin.

But okay, okay, if I really must start from somewhere, let's just say that my parents were cut from a hard-working bench-cloth. Bench-cloth is a type of fabric that had a lot to do with the backbreaking labor of quilting America. The cloth was quite durable, too. And had many useful purposes. Children could be carried in this cloth. Floors could be polished and shined by this cloth. Soldiers got to wear this cloth. The nightlife got to be wooed and dazzled by this cloth. And the whole world slept under this cloth. This cloth was the mother of all cloths.

I'm not making all of this stuff up either. You know, talking that theatrical commercial talk, like the night after *Roots* aired and me suddenly walking around thinking that was our roots too.

I heard about these dexterous bench-cloths with my own ears, and seen't some of them with my own eyes. They were, and are, actual touchable and seeable cloths that fanned out before boxed cameras tailored in bonnets, brogans, boots, and the whole batched bundle of backbreaking goods.

And let me tell you something else too. Most now want a piece of this cloth. The problem is they don't know what it looks like, even when rubbed raw in the face with the cloth. That's because they often mistake it for just another rag.

I don't like dishonesty, so I'ma go on and finish this. Goshladang wasn't playing around when he got to fooling around with the threads sewed through my parents and thus our table. And again, I'm not talking about personalities and likes and dislikes and whatnot. I'm talking about some serious it don't get no better than this DNA tabletop mixing.

I just can't explain it no better than that.

SAYING GRACE

The Scrapbook version: During the making of preparations to attend a family gathering my husband and I got into discussing the trip to head up to Philadelphia where my parents still live. It was a conversation that always took place whenever my husband learned he had to drive anywhere over five miles.

Like all the other times, this time started off no different. My husband needed to know what time I planned to leave, when I planned to return, what the occasion was, if I was taking one bag or two, and so forth and so on.

Basically he was fooling around with the litany of filaments he fooled around with every time he needed to summon an excuse to stay home.

This time his excuse hung around a marital dispute that had erupted within the family. He thought emotions were still running a little too high to get together—the best excuse he had come up with in a long time.

Truth be told, both of us enjoyed the comfort of our brand new suburban environment. The homes, apartments, and condominiums were all brand new. The streets all had recently been paved. The stores and banks were being built between our forty-mile a day drive to and from work where parking, incidentally, was free. None of our neighbors we knew. All of them were new too. Even our plush leather sofa and our wired to a space Canaveral television were brand new. Everything was brand new. Even our attitudes were brand new. We could come into our brand new apartment, close the door, and marinate into our favorite spacious corners of a room not have to hear, feel, or deal with anything we didn't want to hear, feel, or deal with.

That's what made trudging up to Philadelphia such a chore. Both of us hated the traffic and the hundreds of things that went along with the traffic; the torn up roads, the attitudes, and the pumping the gas to get there at a break-neck speed to face a 13" television where we needed a pair of binoculars to watch. But cutting over to Jim's for steaks and hoagies was almost worth the hassle. Well that along with the thawing out out-dated stories we would stuff right back into an icebox to refreeze and then thaw out the next time we drummed up the stamina to make the trip.

But for this particular occasion, I knew my mother. I knew she could care less whether we sat around the table stone-faced, or sat at the table baring our teeth and breathing out of the side of our necks. She wanted all of us to round up our troops and be at her house, which included my husband. As far as she was concerned, all we needed to do was gas up our vehicles and actually get there.

So my husband and I started discussing the trip. It wasn't a big lathery conversation. Actually, it never was. Usually I would ask once, and as soon as the n— met the tip of his tongue, my foot would be on the gas peddle hauling tail out alone.

I would zip on up to Philly and zip right on back, and that would be the end of it. I understood how he felt. If it hadn't been my home, I would have stayed back too. But this time my husband was acting a little peculiar. Usually he hit it and quit it. "No," he wasn't going.

Instead of hitting it and quitting it he got to b-bopping around me and hustling his shoulders as he always did when he was way too excited about something. He was happy, so I knew he was going.

"The trick is," he started off, "is if you can withstand that black table. That black table is a mo' fo'."

A mo' fo'?

Of course I knew what he was talking about. But then again, did I really? No one ever summarized our table quite like that. I knew he wasn't trying to say we needed a new table. That was a beautiful piece of black lacquer sitting in the center of my parent's dining room. Heck, that table came off a sales floor at Bloomingdales. And everybody knows Bloomingdales don't sell junk.

Now, too, he could have been talking about one of the chairs. If I remember correctly, I think one of the legs on one of the chairs was a little uneven. Or was that the floor? I don't think those hardwood floors had been touched since some time in 1930, when the house was built. I definitely know the plastic seat coverings weren't all the best. They were sticky in the summer and cold in the winter. But the seats were white, which worse than sticky or cold seats has to be filthy seats.

Of course I knew why he was keyed up. And so does anyone else who spends a lot of time around water coolers. If there was one discussion a news junkie enthusiast who had to be there at noon, six, and ten didn't want to miss, it would be the discussion that took place at the black table just after a rift in the family had occurred.

But I'm no news junkie enthusiast. I miss all the water cooler talk. What the heck, it's probably about me anyway. And I don't watch the news. Hey look, I'm on my way to work at six, seven, and eight in the morning. Yes, I leave the house at all those times.

At six in the evening I'm on my way home from work—probably somewhere stuck in traffic. And at ten I'm either reading a good book, hopefully writing a good book, on the telephone, or sleep. Take your pick. And no, don't even ask. My radio and ipod only pick up music—all music.

I simply have no need or use for that kind of news. So take it from there, this is not what the black table is about.

At the black table we laugh together, say grace together, eat together, and sometimes yes, we also fight and cry together. I don't know of a wealthier table. Whatever else could sustain a whole family in sickness and in health, for better or for worse, in poverty and through prosperity, and continue to endure. Nothing else but our stories.

Pull up to our table and instantly big dumpling spoonfuls along memory lane is scooped up and served to everyone seated at the table. No bowls are left empty. Everyone must slurp up. All those who want seconds, we add more zing. And for those who comment about how our dishes get zingier, we add more zang. The added zing and extra zang is the whole art in storytelling. This is what gives the stirring flavor and makes a simple memoir legendary.

You see, flexibility in telling stories is a good thing. I mean even, and please sit up straight to hear this, but even serious non-fiction is flexible. All respect due to the educated philosopher, but do you really think an educated guess is infallible to flexibility?

Trust me, if the educated guess was infallible to flexibility, there would be only one fat serious non-fiction book in circulation today. It would be called World-View 1-BC, which incidentally would be a huge relief to students constantly being hit up with costly revised textbooks.

There also would be no breaking news, and no superstars. Although the proverbial white horse would be planked in the center of a field, a whole bunch of us would be a whole lot less convinced and much more open-minded.

Please believe me, memoirs and fiction would take up all of the shelf space in bookstores and libraries. The only other genre in the store would be a copy of the World-View 1-BC book. As soon as you walked in the door that book would be screwed to the reference desk.

Not that anyone could, but bookstores and libraries wouldn't want anyone hauling away the most important book in the world.

At our table we love telling stories. That's what we mostly do. We sit around telling stories. Some of the stories really happened as it's spelled out. That being, no one disagrees with the version. And then… well… oh well, and then some of the stories are just one side of an imagination.

Innocently enough however, my father was our black table's architect. I say innocently enough because it was my father who just so happened loved talking. When I say he knew everything, I am not exaggerating.

He knew how to read his body and could tell when something was wrong. He was the one who had to tell the doctor his appendices were about to rupture, or else the doctor wouldn't have know until maybe it was too late. He could read behavior and knew all about insects and rodents and could talk all night long about politics.

Consequently, it was he who got us to communicating. Had it not been for his daily presence at our table, and his stubborn dogmatic insistence to do things his way, ultimately structuring our family, we would have never come upon this powerful table. We would have never understood the value in talking about it. And we would have never known there was such a resilient influence that could sustain us forever; in sickness and in health, for better or for worse, and in poverty and through prosperity. Our black table is a mo fo' alright.

It is to this end that I unveil our black table with a typical rendition of Mr. Clarke.

LITTLE RUSTY WALLACE

My father, Mr. Clarke, is a man who cares much about his family. I would like to extend my father's caring to include all people, however because my father has great difficulty understanding human behavior, his passion for people is somewhat limited. He expands his border of love no broader than our black table.

None-the-less, as *a way to beat all ironies* has its way of dealing a pretty comical hand, my father ended up in his early-retirement years embarking on a teaching career; certainly out of necessity—so add no love there. I mean, I really wished I could rave on about how my father went for working with children in the public school system out of love, or maybe even out of devotion for helping young people, or our society or something, but this just wasn't the case.

My father simply was out of a job. But even so, my father still is an honorable man. He is an honorable man who believes in standards. The way he sees it, if laws are made, then for the most part those laws should be adhered to.

So here is this man who believes in family and standards, but knowing little about human behavior. Therefore, this leaves a gaping hole around his concern for others. Yet my father is working in the Philadelphia public school system, taking roll one morning for a class he is 'subbing'. Subbing means he is a substitute teacher.

For the first few days while subbing a first grade class my father calls out names on a roll sheet. He finds one name on the roll sheet that belongs to a student who has never shown up in class. Now the rule in this particular school was that any student who missed school for more than three consecutive days, that student's name had to be submitted to the attendance office so that the student could either be located, or dropped from the roster.

My father did as instructed and reported this student as a no show for the three consecutive days. When the student's name continued to show up on the roster, my father took additional steps to make the attendance office was aware of the erroneous name on the roll sheet. Eventually after some persistence the name was removed.

Now, the roll sheet was not my father's only concern. He takes the entire subbing role seriously. So not only does he adhere to the standards of taking roll, but he goes an extra mile by making it his business to walk out to the schoolyard and monitor the children lining up for class.

I guess the best way to put it, my father cares about the job. And in caring about the job, though he is slow to admit it, he really cares about the children. So I am going to go on and put it out there. My father really has a desire to love others. Now, you can go on and add a whole lot of love here.

One morning my father notices an older man pushing a young child in line with the students lining up for his class. He sees this, but doesn't give it much deliberation. There are thirty other students he also is looking after.

He walks the students to class, and like every morning, commences taking roll. All the children, except one, raise their hand after their name is called. My father looks at the little boy who never raised his hand and asked him his name. The little boy said his name was, let's say, Rusty Wallace. It was the same name on the roll sheet he's spent days trying to have removed from the roster. And it was the same child who the old man had shoved in line.

"Oh, so you are Rusty Wallace," he says.

In a soliloquy tiring to the most energetic toastmaster, he proceeded to explain to the child how he couldn't just show up in school. He tells the child that he must go to the office and be admitted to school. But then midway into the soliloquy he realizes he is talking to a child who has no idea what he talking about. He; instead, informs the office about the child's sudden appearance.

But then, after my father and the school administrators go through a number of hoops to have the child's name added to the roster, the following few days little Rusty Wallace doesn't show up in class. Once again my father must commence to reporting little Rusty as a no show for some odd consecutive amount of days. This back and forth row goes on for a couple of days when, just as the roster issue gets settled, one morning the old man is found once more pushing little Rusty in line again.

That morning my father was unable to catch the old man, so little Rusty sat in class with his name hanging in limbo. The following day Rusty was out of school, following by the next few days thereafter. My father found himself back to reporting the child as a no show, when yet again, one morning there was the old man pushing little Rusty in line. That time my father caught the old man.

"Hey, look my man, you can't just bring this child to school whenever you feel like it. This child must attend school regularly; every day. You need to take him to the office to have him readmitted."

"Sir, I am the grandfather," the man contended. "I can't take him to the office," he says turning away and heading in an opposite direction.

My father doesn't give in. Doing his best to keep the old man and child together, he further explains, and forcefully no less, "It's no excuse. This child needs to be in class every day. This is how school works. My man, you're going to have to take him to the office to have him readmitted."

"But we don't have a home, and it's hard for me to get him here every day," the old man pleads.

My father is stunned. This is the first time he has personally been forced to face this type of problem. Aided by a whole lot of missing information, everyone he knows, at the very least, has a place to lay their head; a place they call home.

My father has no idea of the debilitating strains placed on the homeless, or what being homeless even means. Sure he's heard of homelessness, but its far-reaching circumstances are well outside of his plaid day-to-day reasoning.

All my father knows is that people should rise early, get dressed appropriately, go to work, or go look for work, work hard, come home, eat, do that thing we all do, and then sleep. For him there's not much else to life, except talking about those who don't practice these habits in the exact order as so laid out.

The old man's story sends my father's reasoning into a tailspin. My father didn't know how to respond, but he had to say something.

"Look, go to the office and explain to them just what you have said to me. They can do something to help you because this child needs to be in school."

A day or so went by when one morning little Rusty Wallace appeared in the schoolyard. Before my father could take note of the child, the old man descended upon him.

Overwhelmed, the old man embraced my father in a bear hug, profusely thanking him. Those few words my father had imparted had gone beyond getting an old man and young child off the streets. Those few words had reset and warmed two old weathered hearts. From that day until my father was reassigned, little Rusty Wallace showed up to class.

CHAPTER TWO

"Einstein's Cobblestones"

Whippin' Machine

Things governing children were a whole lot different in the seventies. The seventies were at the tip end of an era where parents didn't take up for their children like today. Parents respected authority and kids feared it. Grown-ups, they were called, could still tell on us and get us in trouble. And authority like school administrators and teachers could twist our ears, wash our mouths out with soap, and snatch our arms out of our arm sockets if we acted up. Authority still wore the iron glove, which was none more true for many teachers who had the right to paddle any student they saw fitting for a paddling.

It didn't matter whether the teacher may have been biased or ignorant of certain facts for why he or she felt it necessary to discipline a student. It didn't matter whether the teacher's sexual orientation was questionable. It mattered none whether or not the teacher had been cruel to animals, or even whether or not the teacher had a past of any sort—pedophile or otherwise. The school board consecrated all teachers with the sovereign power and right to administer discipline to whomever they so deemed necessary to get in line. And Miz Cussins I like calling her, a woman who I remember giving real meaning to the beehive look, leveraged her corporal punishment allotment to the fullest extent of her certified teaching unlimited limitations.

Whipalcoholic Miz Cussins, or the Whipalcoholic I will refer to her throughout, with the spider woman thick black-framed glasses, roach killer shoes, and Strawbridge tailored suits made to fit her trim figure-eight frame to a tee, tore up a many of tails in her way back in the day whipping days. The woman never taught me, and I am positive she didn't even know I existed, but her name got around to every student who attended Pastorius back then. The Whipalcoholic was one whipping triple-A machine.

My brother had the Whipalcoholic for a teacher, so not only should he have known about her reputation, he did know about her reputation. But my brother was a bit of a hardhead, something like me. The only difference between us was that I would have never tested someone who had the capacity to be remembered as the Whipalcoholic. Perhaps I was a little smarter. I knew who to play with, and who to avoid. I knew darn well there wasn't no out-smarting a whipalcoholic.

But my brother thought different. It was either that, or he just wasn't thinking at all when he revved up the audacity to tell the Whipalcoholic that the reason he didn't complete a homework assignment was because our parents told him we didn't have to do homework when we had company.

Why o why my brother didn't complete the homework assignment to begin with, especially when all of his classmates had, begs the main question. But why o why he used this lie is the real million dollar eye-popping question. You'd have to either be not very bright, which my brother was quite intelligent, or totally zoned out to come up with this excuse.

Now back in this day I dare even insinuate that my brother was zoned out, zoned out. To be that kind of zoned out would mean he had to be on something like drugs, which he was not. Well, not unless those Flintstone vitamins he chewed a whole bottle of could be included as a drug. But he sure had backed himself into some kind of a peculiar brain twisting zone to come up with this lie.

The Whipalcoholic didn't even call my parents. She didn't have to. My parents were well known by administrators, faculty, and staff. Back then they were all going by first names. The Whipalcoholic knew without losing one eyelash my parents would have never said such a thing. There simply was no need to confirm what she already knew. This was one reason; one main reason teachers were granted this chastising power.

The Whipalcoholic, one teacher who had absolutely zero tolerance for recalcitrant children, handled her business like any woman of high authority in charge of disobedience. She quickly acquainted an outright lying child with her number one assistant—a yardstick with more inches on it than the tallest child in class.

The Whipalcoholic was trying to save a generation of children from becoming lost. I'm sure that's how she probably saw it. She was helping our economy. Out of hand children weren't only a menace to themselves and their parents. They wreaked havoc on the economy. Everyone ended up paying a price for undisciplined children.

My father felt the same way. Like the Whipalcoholic's style, my father praised the military's style of discipline too. He said drill instructors and platoon leaders didn't need a smart triple-A whippersnapper all the way in foreign territory asking questions because he or she wasn't ready yet. When it was time to lock and load, it was time to lock and load. Later for all the what for and I'm busy right now. And yeah, sometimes it made no sense to order a soldier to the breaking rocks detail, but that was the whole point. Discipline was the name of the game. Taking orders and asking questions later.

See, had the World 1-BC book been written all of this would have already been laid out. No one would be sitting around asking questions and saying this was all wrong. Cruelty administered for no other purpose other than to be mean was wrong. But keeping folks in line to bring about order and civility so that whole country wasn't running into one another was right.

Talk about seeing flying dinosaurs and rafters of bricks shivering and buckling, mess around with the Whipalcoholic. I'm saying blink, and before you knew it dusk would have turned to daylight. The Whipalcoholic didn't play. It usually didn't take more than one sassy attitude to straighten out an entire schoolyard of students.

The Whipalcoholic simply told my brother to go get his sister. Now right here my brother was given a second chance. He could have gotten me. I was just about, or maybe even more so recalcitrant than he was, and... I was his sister too. I probably would have turned in my good common sense just to get him out of a pinch.

But no, my brother wasn't thinking about me. This had to be about the very moment he had wised up. Of course he knew which sister the Whipalcoholic was referring to. The

Whipalcoholic was referring to our Ms. Goody Two Shoes sister. As I said earlier, these teachers weren't consecrated with this whipping power absentmindedly. They were conferred this power judiciously.

My brother, all wised up, went on and recited the only prayer that had probably worked miracles for him on other occasions. You know the prayer. It's the last resort prayer bearing a few of the most prominent words in a prayer… "God please help me."

This was the prayer my brother must have recited as he nervously concentrated on how he was going to get my sister to dig him out of the mess he had dug himself into. Heading toward the Whipalcoholic's classroom my brother kept telling my sister, "…just say yes." Everyone has heard the slogan, "Just Say No." Well this was where it came from. My brother telling my sister, "…just say yes." Over and over he kept telling her this.

See, now right here I would have known right off the bat what my brother meant. Never mind the perfect campaign slogan everyone by now knows to strike. I would have read all between the lines, back and forth over the lines, the lines upside down and right side up, and known that my brother was knee deep in it. But you see, people like my sister don't have any business reading things like the handwriting on the wall. Iffy billboards and vacillating marketing schemes aren't what they are good at interpreting. It's just not their specialty. They need all the print enlarged and in bold font.

My sister walked into the Whipalcoholic's classroom instantly greeted with, "Alecia, do your parents tell you that you don't have to do homework when you have guest over?"

"Huh?"

See, I told you. My sister didn't have to utter another syllable. And the whipalcoholic needed to ask no more questions. True to the Whipalcoholic's reputation, she handled my brother like she handled all the other licentiousness children before him. With one well-trained aim, and a yardstick in feets' one way and inches the other, came from way back sending my brother sailing across the classroom.

Now that was exactly the way homework got done back in the day.

The Incubator

And then too, sometimes the pendulum swung the other way. Looking the other way our parents did exactly as the master of rearing well-disciplined children had prescribed.

They fed us, bathed us, clothed us, talked to us, read to us, and didn't whip the daylights out of us or exploit us sexually. They used all the variables that promised to turn perfect children into decent adults. The only variable they missed was the variable that swung the pendulum the other way.

But nearly all parents miss at least one variable. It's the variable covered under the laws of motion. You know the variable. It's the variable that says there is no such thing as a perfect parent.

Our parents pledged their allegiance to one faithful old school rule, "because I said so". Because I said so alone was going to take us a long ways.

Because I said so was going to help us maintain great posture, mind our manners, and get us through college and onto good employment. When we had a thought, because I said so spoke. And if we didn't have a thought, because I said so still spoke. Today I tease my parents all the time about how if we were too cold, how we would look at one another moving solely our eyes, mumbling to each other.

"Are you cold?"

"Yes I'm cold."

"Are you cold?"

We wouldn't dare open our mouths to let the author of temperature, obviously a figure of absolute because I said so authority, know how we felt. That was because I said so's duty.

Even if because I said so didn't know how we felt,

because I said so always knew how we were supposed to feel. And because I said so always knew just what to say.

Looking back however, my mother laughs about how we should have froze. She says we were fools. She never waited for someone to speak up for her. She always spoke up for herself. And she could be speaking to anyone, of any tenor too.

Umm... but not us.

She didn't have herself for a mother. Shucks, we would stand side-by-side shivering out in the cold until even hell froze over.

That was exactly how my sister and I tiptoed into Muzon's lane on this blistery cold winter day. I think we were getting our hair done for Easter. Both of us showed up at this homespun beauty shop very short on pleasantries, with a full head of long, thick, resolute chocolate hair.

Usually my mother fussed over our bountiful beautiful body of hair. Unless we were spending the summer with our Southern relatives whose hair we seemed to have plagiarized, or like the one time when my mother had taken ill, would she allow someone other than herself to fool around with our hair. But for this special occasion, whatever it was, she let loose those reigns. She turned those reigns over to two women who were like the original authors of temperature.

My mother didn't even turn the motor to the car off.

She just pulled up to the curb, tossed us a good-sized book of instructions, and went on about her way. She'd see us in a few hours. That's how long she estimated we would be in the place.

And so, there. With respect to children, that's how decisions were made. No consulting, or reasoning, or advising even. You didn't have to like it, but you had to take it... exactly how we ended up in the shotgun homespun salon very short on pleasantries.

I'ma go on and call the place Muzon, only because Ms. Ebony's, which even that wasn't the name of the salon, sounds too cozy for a hole in the wall where the character light needs to be lit up to describe.

You see, Muzon denotes the ominous, toothy, and cumbersome look the steel fixtures, cracked vinyl chairs, checkered linoleum floors, short despondent lights, and tall orders short on pleasantries gave off.

I remember standing in the center of Muzon's ebonyville feeling friendless and uninvited, even though I know my mother made an appointment. There was not a stir or sound around. No music playing, no telephone ringing, no humming coming from any of the fixtures, or popping of gum even. There was plain, straight up, no nothing. It was just my sister, and then I, guessing what was next.

At some point we must have been shoved into a chair because there I sat leafing through my brain. I couldn't figure out how in the world I was going to relay the cumbersome instructions my mother had given us to recite to the tall orders short on pleasantries.

I mean, these tall orders came super-sized—you know, not off the child menu. They had the type of attitudes that met customers at the door: 'Want Customer Service? Do your own nappy head!'

In other words, beyond the x,y,z sequence of instructions, wasn't a darn 'nother thing coming out of our mouths. A 'this is what my mother said she wanted done' in any language, made good sense not to repeat. Telling anyone that later could be referred to as a Muzon 'to do this and do that', but my mother said, 'don't do this and don't do that' was saying way too much.

If my mother didn't like the 'this and the that', then she could corner the aftermath of the 'this and the that' after the 'this and the that' had transpired. But I think we said something. We must have said something because after that, this is what happened:

For an exhausting space in time we sat on cracked vinyl chairs with a mean piece of black beaten tarp draped around our torsos, waiting. We both waited our turn to meet our hair fixer-upper fate.

To this day I don't recall what all of the steps involved in the hair fixing process were, but when our mother fixed our hair she never had us sitting in crack vinyl chairs with an ugly black tarp draped around us. And we never sat before an ominous black curtain that looked to lead into the deep dark unknown. That much I do recall... and then some.

The tallest order, a big burlap of doom and gloom, was on duty first. The big burlap of doom and gloom was what could be referred to as the shampoo girl. But in this case... well in this case, dilute the shampoo and scratch off the girl. Hey, I can't recall smelling shampoo, and I never saw the girl. All I recall seeing was an order so tall on gloom I was afraid to look up.

I kept my head down as the big burlap of doom and gloom commanded my sister to follow her behind the black curtain that lead into the deep dark unknown. The entire time my sister was behind the curtain, I wondered what in the world was going on. I really thought my sister was being exposed to a secret that would never be privy to me. I thought my sister was going to emerge from behind the curtain with the 'ha ha, I'm not telling' expression sprawled across her face. Just what in the heck was going on behind the black curtain, I was anxious to know.

I heard no sounds, but when my sister finally appeared from behind the mysterious curtain, I noticed her eyes were a little red, and she looked at me a little strange. But before she could sit beside me, and I could sneak all of my unanswered questions out of her, the big burlap of doom and gloom had burrowed down on me. It was my turn. I was finally going to get my turn to see what was behind the black curtain leading to the deep dark unknown.

Man, oh man. I walked into a small cramped room more spiritless than the black curtain. The only light fed into the room came from a very tiny window, which the big burlap of doom and gloom was positioned in front of. You know what I am saying. No light was getting in that room.

In all this misery I, to this very day, don't know how in all of the Christmas lights that can ever light up Christmas Eve, made out the two black sink bowls, the black vinyl chairs, and the gray shelves filled with old gray towels. Right then something told me I had better get to praying.

I eased back into the chair and instinctively closed my eyes. In one swift motion, which I could feel even with my eyes shut tight, four squares of toilet tissue being whipped around my neck, and two bear claws of envy snatching up a chunk of my hair; my plethora bounty of beautiful long, thick, resolute chocolate hair.

At this point it seemed that I would have instinctively opened my eyes, but nope. Instinctively I squeezed my eyes even tighter together as the bear claws of pitilessness that could choke the crap out of ten grizzlies at once, yanked and pulled, banged and punched and beat my head around a dime-sized sink bowl. My prayer quickly wrapped up its beginning begging whiny verse and threw me the Jaws of Life. I clamped down on knowing good and well that grizzly knew its damn strength.

Had this winch lost her mind?

But what could I have said... what should I have said... "Ouch?"

After the stressed out grizzly released me, and I emerged from behind the black curtain, I am sure my eyes, probably even more so than my sister's eyes since I had more hair to contend with, were beet red too.

I looked over at my sister, who was staring intently into my eyes, and said with my own eyes of course, "is that what happened to you?"

Other than laughing about the shampoo job outside the ear shot of the hole in the wall; you know after our plethora bounty of beautiful long, thick, resolute chocolate hair had been sizzled up to our necks, we never spoke of the incident until... well until we reached the point that the only part of the seesaw we were ever going to ride again, was the up part—the end result of emerging from submissiveness.

LOVE ON THE BLACK HAND SIDE

Back braces and leg crutches aside, every time, anytime, and all day long I want the parents who would do everything for me, except seeing things my way, their way.

The curtain flew up for us one warm evening in California while we—my father, my mother, my sister, my brother, and myself—were on a two-week sunny-side up vacation. It was the farthest we had been away on a vacation. And not that this had anything to do with the curtain flying up, but flying 3000 miles away to a place that actually looked like 3000 miles away from where we had come, can be disruptive to the psyche when something like a curtain suddenly flies up.

Back in the seventies, vacationing in Los Angeles was like living in Madrid, even though I have never been to Spain. But that's the whole point. This vacation was like a living dream. We went swimming. We played tennis. We burned up on Magic Mountain. We drove along Rodeo Drive, ooed and awed in and out of Beverly Hills, stood in a few of the stars shoes, went out dining, and then one evening while my mother was hanging out with her sisters, my father got the fitting notion to show us a little more of paradise.

Oh boy. In the midst of vacationing in this wonderful, wonderful wonderland of a utopia where everything was glitter and sunshine, and fancy and new, my father out of the clear blue decided he was taking us to see a movie. The three of us had not a clue what the movie was going to be about. Chitty-Chitty Bang Bang, or maybe it was Pearl Harbor, was the last movie we had seen together as a family. And since my father got all the say so, we naturally assumed the movie would fall along his lines.

Blithely we expected the movie would either something historical classic, or something Rated G classy. Whatever the movie, we knew my father was a responsible father who exposed us to responsible fatherly-standardized things. Never would contaminants more lethal than him be freely breezing around our sphere at his invite. Bits and pieces of that real-life trauma we had to siphon from outside the walls of our home, or from practical imagination.

So when my father said, "we're going to see a movie, let's go," we simply jumped into our sneakers and made no assumptions about the possibility of a low-budget curtain being a part of our surprise.

We walked to the movie theatre skipping along the unbroken pavement behind my father, excited and thrilled about another adventure tossed our way. And again, let me reiterate, it was a beautiful evening. The sun was setting just like so, hanging an ever-glowing magnificent red-orange fireball light over the city. The palms sang to us along the way, fanning us left and right. The recently cemented ashy white sidewalk ran like chalky butterscotch beneath our feet. And everyone walking by moved along in rhythm with the mood the Hollywoodish ambience the west side of Inglewood comfortably pulled off.

We arrived at the movie theatre where the lights from the street, the sky, and the theatre all met up, coloring in the rest of our night. It was nothing like back home, a claustrophobic cold familiar dingy unidentifiable gray. This was LA at its finest. My father purchased the movie tickets and we skipped right on behind him, following him into the theater.

The seats in the theater were the best. The red cushiony leather-like seats looked brand new. They looked like something I wanted to jump up and down on to see how high I could bounce. But then the last time I had that inkling I remembered the radiator almost taking me out when my father caught me in the midst of my highest bounce. I settled instead on plopping my butt in the chair to get a little bounce from the cushion that way.

Oh wait! I forgot the treats. Now, how could I forget the treats? Yes, my father splurged on popcorn, candy, and soft drinks for us too. We didn't even have to look over at the concession stand. He beat our glowing subdued eyes getting over to the glass case. Before we knew it, Twizzlers and Snowball Chocolates were in our hands, and we didn't even like Twizzlers or Snowball Chocolates.

Back to the theatre—a theatre football-field size huge where rows and rows, and more rows of these red cushioned seats lined the auditorium. All I saw was red seats, amplified and magnified by high ceilings and arena lighting. Whoever had to change the light bulbs had to have a PhD in light bulb changing. Wasn't no light bulb changing manual going to help whoever had to climb that high to change that many light bulbs. There had to be a million of those little lights up there.

Then the theatre lights dimmed and a bitch lost her coat. I think it was just about then when the seats started filling in. Maybe this was how I missed the opening pitch of the movie—looking and bouncing around.

The first part of the movie just seemed a little slow. There was some flat old-school city-type action going on where the plot seemed jumbled between a jitter-bug in a jittery get-up with a slick ride, and a hip-hop sista' with a real bitching type of attitude. Yeah, it was a real slow start. The film looked a whole lot like something I'd seen back home. Nothing to really sink my teeth in and say, "oh, wow." It was just enough to look at and maybe say, "oh, yeah."

...oops, and then somebody on screen cursed. Yes, somebody had a funky foul mouth. Somebody used a profane word, and not that I had never heard the word. It's just I had never heard the word on screen before. I hadn't heard much more than damn on screen. People just didn't talk like that out in the open. The words flipping off the screen were the type of words that had my mind going, 'Oool, did you hear that?'

I didn't turn to look at my sister. Not just yet. I was so busy digesting the profanity. And then, just before I could fully swallow the dialogue, was it when I heard more profanity... again and again, and more profane and just a plain damn shame. At some point the profane words started shuffling behind the mother. You know, the mother followed by a bunch of Bae-Bae's little string of rug rats.

Oh boy, these characters on screen had mouths full of puss. My eyes were growing bigger and bigger every tenth of a second. The puss just oozed out of their mouths... all of their mouths. Instinctively I remember thinking, we shouldn't be seeing this... should we? It was like... well it was like a forbidden curtain had been snatched up. Way up. Gee whiz, it reached the point where I was having difficulty trying to distinguish between what was really vulgar, and just plain vulgar.

Before I could turn to confirm my thoughts with my sister, the legs of the woman with the bitching role went up in the air. Instantly, I jumped. It wasn't only a whole lot of leg, but damn, it really was a whole lot of leg. And these legs were spread as far apart as I had never seen two legs spread apart. The lady had to have been an acrobat. That was how my mind was racing.

Just when the lady's legs could spread no further, JD plummeted down on her with his daddy's revenge. Oh man, without taking another guess I snatched around to face my sister, who also snatched around at the same moment to face me. Our faces had to be wearing identical expressions of disbelief. It was a good thing we weren't holding the soft drink.

Our mother would have never taken us to see such a picture, and if our father had any sense, he would have rounded us up and got us the hell out of there. That's how we were thinking. We peeked over at my father, who was staring straight at the screen, and then turned back around looking starstruck at each other again.

"Oh my God!"

That's how our mouths were moving, even though no words were ever exchanged. We never looked at each other again. We simply sat back, numbly popping popcorn in our mouths, and dropping Twizzlers and Snowball Chocolates on the floor, while JD finished tearing somebody's ass up—right on screen.

Pink Floyd

The last people we wanted to see up at our school were one of our parents. My brother nearly passed out dead smack in the middle of his 'got damn', when he looked up and saw my father wild eyed, clenched teeth, and fist knotted up tighter than lint on knit coming across the schoolyard towards him.

Same thing with my sister. She slid down in her seat and covered her eyes when she looked up and saw my mother barreling into the classroom wrapped in a brown bear coat with a rainbow tie-died scarf tied around her head. That was the last time she forgot her lunch.

I was the same way, too. I caught my heart skipping and dancing around the floor when I looked up and saw my father entering my classroom. He looked mad as hell. Had me trying to figure out what I was doing just before he walked in. I totally forgot about how bitterly I complained about the class I was in.

But that's how we were. We didn't want the white-collar father wearing the neckties and suits with the London Fogs tossed over an arm showing up in the middle of class. And neither did we want the practical mother who was more concerned about dressing properly for the weather, than she was about how she looked interrupting class either.

It just wasn't cool having those types of parents. We wanted the cool parents who our friends would fall for and think were cool too. Now, of course we never expressed any of this outwardly. Just as we certainly didn't go out of our way to stir them up and have them snooping around school making sure no one was doing us wrong.

Looking back, I guess we weren't putting two-and-two together. Just like the RE (remedial education) class I didn't feel I belonged in. After my mother ignored me hanging onto the door handle refusing to go in the classroom, I pretty much accepted my fate. By week two I was sharing a brand new funny classroom story every other night. That's what had my father up at the school looking mad as hell. He wanted me out of the class, and immediately. But at least he could have warned me. I'm sure I would have stopped sharing those "guess what Herman did today" stories.

But that's how it was at the table back then. We would laugh and toss our little stories up in the air thinking that's just where they would stay; up in the air. Unless the situation was extremely serious, such as the night a group of boys snatched my sister's Halloween bag, would we expect our parents to respond. There wasn't any guessing about whether our parents were listening or not when my sister was screaming like a ten alarm red-engine fire. We fully expected our father to burst through the front door and run off into the night after the bag snatchers, which was exactly what he did.

But what can I say? Maybe we were a little slow. It took a while to realize our parents were listening to, and ingesting, everything that came out of our mouths. But while this while was taking a while, stories like these were happening all the time...

...one of us at the table talking about some of the neighborhood hoodlums taking money off younger kids. Gold snatching and lunch money taking was a sign of the times back there in the seventies where we lived.

Though we weren't the stick-up kid, one of us had to have been sharing some other child's personal misfortune. But our parents never said a word. My father might have been sucking his teeth however, something he did when he was angry, but the point is, I never recalled the moment when my father threw the dinner napkin in his plate and snatched away from the table saying he had had enough. And my mother never grabbed his arm and told him to please calm down. None of this never happened.

The very next day it had to have been, we left school—each of us at separate times—thinking nothing of our discussion at the table the day before. My brother left school with the little rowdy crowd he hung around. My sister left school with her little Huxtable looking friends. And I, as usual, left school alone.

All of us however, at separate points heading downhill past Awbury Park, saw the huge crowd congregating at the bottom of the hill. It was a monumental energy of cheers and jubilation none of us could miss, regardless of where we were on the hill.

"It's a fight! It's a fight!"

Three pm fair-ones were still fairly common back then. That's when classmates settled beefs; out of earshot and out of sight of faculty and staff.

To say the least, the unrest at the bottom of the hill looked like one of those 3pm fair ones that were going to be the talk of school for rest of the year. It looked like a gang of hornets spraying the park. Somebody had stepped on somebodies toes accidentally and hadn't said excuse me. We could count on three or four fights like that every school year.

The excitement was amped up so high I think someone even looped their arms in mine and pulled me along too.

"Come on. Come on. It's a fight! It's a fight!"

Now, despite what it may have looked like, I wasn't all the way thrilled. It wasn't unheard of to be racing to see a fight and learn the crowd was waiting for you. Maybe I had stepped on someone's toes and didn't know it. I hardly wanted to come upon my own surprise any more than I cared to see two boys sparing Cassius Clay style, or a couple of females rolling around the ground pulling at each other's hair and stripping each other down to underwear.

My heart skipped a few paces as I raced downhill hoping the fight would turn out to be all smoke and no fire. Occasionally that turned out to be the case too. A whole lot of huffing and puffing, but no kicking up dirt and flames.

As I spiraled downhill at the discretion of the crowd pulling and pushing around me, my intention was to somehow get around the crowd and get home. Hey, it was perfectly cool being the one mannequin at the back of the classroom who hadn't seen or heard anything.

Just like that, my one wish was granted. A path opened up wide enough for ten brides all swathed in yards and yards of fancy Priscilla fabrics to walk through. That was funny too. Normally banded together hornets weren't so charitable with space. It took a little squeezing and nudging the tiniest of air pockets getting through those types of nests.

I would be lying if I tried explaining where my heart had skipped off to at that point. My only sense of ease was in the gaping hole that had fanned out around me. Someone had called a 3pm fair one, but no one was there.

Standing in this open area, and it's no exaggeration, in a no breathing room park full of people—it looked as if I called the fight and my adversary had chickened out. That wasn't so good either. A no show adversary didn't necessarily mean that would be the end of the story.

Synchronized with me trying to put the picture together I heard my brother calling me. He was sort of hissing at me, discreetly trying to get my attention. I looked over at him puzzled, at the same time someone in the crowd shouted, "Hey, isn't that your father!"

Good grief. We skirted on home shielding our eyes from police officers approaching on horseback, the neighborhood hoodlums who were from a side of the family no one supposedly liked, and a marvelous crowd cheering on a man sporting the white dress shirt, necktie, and a London Fog draped over one arm.

No Place Like Home

The chain of command we followed was first my father, and then my mother. My father was the first in command because he did all of the prophesizing, the analyzing, the theorizing, and vocalizing. He had the military background, so he was the platoon leader; in charge of us all.

It was he who learned regulations on how to pull sheets on a bed so tight a quarter could bounce on it. It was he who caught flying bats with his bare hands when everyone else in the office had run off like the building was on fire. It was he who peeled a million potatoes in one sitting, without asking one question. It was he who ran all those laps around Lackland's Air Base... in ten seconds... backwards.

He was so disciplined he could eat an eight-course meal in five seconds flat, drop the plate at the sound of a whistle, and be ready for the next drill. And even if I am exaggerating, don't think I am making fun of him either. No, not at all. All of us, to include my mother and a lot of other people too, looked way up to him. We believed he could move a mountain if ever a mountain needed moving.

Everyday, all day, every day of the year he had our attention. Lucky for my mother, she can now rest on her uncontaminated laurels on not having to be credited for gadgets he created and spearheaded, and drilled right through the ground.

One gadget he came up with, the one we ceremoniously give him full credit, was our family discussion hour. There would be no Black Table had not this discussion hour been invented. Every Sunday after dinner he set aside an hour for us to air our concerns; to speak up and speak out, in so many words.

I will admit this family discussion hour creeping over a restricted horizon got my eyes to growing real big like. I was like, "awl Daddy finally came around. Look at Daddy reaching out to reach us. At last Daddy finally was going to put the Air Force to bed and see things our way. See, he wasn't so stubborn and tough after all."

Yes, slap the one big red X on me. I was sold.

The next thing I knew—Attention!—The horizon caved in and creeping over a horizon had blown up to—AT EASE. I should have known.

For thirty minutes or more our family discussion hour jumped off with my father preaching more of his beliefs, and highlighting more of his trophies. This drill instructor wasn't turning in his bugle after all. He was going to blow and blow and blow on that bugle, until blow blew up. All I can say is the Air Force surely got a hold of him. They had him blowing that canton at 0-nepalm hour every morning, and now he was going to be blowing his bugle right through dinner, too.

The worst part of the discussion was that we first had to sit through the introduction of him going ballistic about flies, mice, and rats and whatnot, to tossing us around 1920, even though he hadn't been born until 1940. Nat Turner's rampage almost always ended up somewhere in the James Weldon Johnson Projects, which all of this might have been okay if at least once we could have said, "awl, this soapbox stuff is smooth sailing working."

But we couldn't, because it wasn't.

The only thing we saw working was that bugle.

While he preached, each of us waited to be cued on when it was our turn to speak. I usually went first. I liked going first because I hated hearing rhetoric. Truthfully, even back then I saw most of what I see today. The ends to all this rhetoric just never seemed to meet. In other words, Goshladang had rhetoric all meshed out. The balancing act of it all kept the draft moving evenly in both directions; up and down, and back and forth.

So badly I wanted to spread out a canvas and paint this balancing picture in motion, but all I had to say was I, and Mr. Rhetoric would dice that one word up until *I* had become I don't give a damn no more. After the first discussion session I realized saving Metropolis wasn't my mission. This made future discussion hours easy for me. I would just sit there and look at Mr. Rhetoric until rhetoric ran out of rhetoric... you know, because I just didn't give a damn anymore.

My sister usually followed me. She always got in a few words beyond my *I*. But Mr. Rhetoric would cut her in a cazillion million little pieces, too. I believe he got the most joy out of slicing and dicing up my sister. Because she always fought back, or at least tried to fight back, it was his opportunity to really challenge his debating tactics. It was where the ends to his beliefs came together—made sense, if you will. Back then I used to feel so sorry for her. She fought so hard. The lop-sided discussion between her and him usually lasted five-minutes; maybe 4.59 seconds longer than my session.

My brother always went last. Now this was the part of our discussion I never wanted to miss. Mr. Rhetoric and this child would go on and on, usually well beyond the stipulated hour time limit. This child would sit there upchucking whatever was at the top of his throat.

Stuff like "the sky is green and bald-headed" or "I like my beef cut from a huge head of cabbage" was the racket this child drummed up. And Mr. Rhetoric sat right there dissecting his argument as if he was painting over a canvas that looked blackened out when I worked on it, but came in sharp as a Leonardo Last Supper portrait when the child touched it.

Oooh… that child used to really get beneath my skin. He could get away with saying, and sometimes doing almost anything, and Mr. Rhetoric rationalized his behavior.

Well one Sunday night we cleared the table to begin our usual dissecting discussions. I believe it was like the second or third Sunday of holding such discussions. I forgot to add; this Sunday discussion stuff didn't last very long. It may have carried on for about two or three Sundays, certainly not many more. As a matter of fact, the particular Sunday I'm about to lay out on the line was the last Sunday we held such a discussion hour.

As usual, I went first. To be fair however, I will admit I offered a little more than *I*. But I will also be honest. Whatever I said, it was no more than one sentence; one sentence something in the area of, "I think these discussions are pointless." Of course I didn't have to add any more. A bug fat sloppy period was put to the beginning of my thought with one solid minute of irate ranting.

He next turned to my sister. Now if I was her I might have passed at that point, but poor child... she jumped right in the center of his noose arguing about why he chose to chop on her. He snatched her right up too, just as he did on all of the other Sundays. I think he even snatched up my mother, who chimed in to help. To the last thumbnail he pounded on both my mother and sister until two nails had become one dimpled thumbnail.

The child was up next.

By this time I had finished clearing the table. It was my dish night. I had stacked all the dishes in the sink, making all the room in the world for Mr. Rhetoric to stretch out and lean back, and enjoy his child's tartlet opening talking about how he didn't like how my parents were raising him.

But wait... wasn't this just about what I had said? I wanted to break the table in two.

But hey, anybody got a Cuban cigar? Mr. Rhetoric looked so satisfied. And I would have been so satisfied too. If only I could have bunched and ruffled that child up and made a messy ascot out of him, and then wrapped him around Mr. Rhetoric's neck until my arms fell off.

While Mr. Rhetoric sat there sucking on a toothpick and his teeth, I rubbed those dishes raw listening. Oooh! Scouring those pots and pans without a scouring pad never felt so good. It was just what I needed to keep from scouring a hole through the wall.

The child plowed on, mowing up things like how he wanted to hang out late, drink wine, smoke weed and stuff like that. Mr. Rhetoric hadn't belched once. He just sat there chewing on that mess, while me on the other side of the wall washing dishes, cheered the child on. I prayed hard that child would pull up the floorboards and really sock it to Mr. Rhetoric. Well, not physically of course, but I wanted to see what rhetoric looked like turned inside out.

Not everyone wanted what Mr. Rhetoric wanted. Just maybe, some of those vagrants he pointed out were a whole lot happier steering their own fate, than he was bawling about the countless enemies steering his fate. I guess what I really wanted, was for Mr. Rhetoric to hear us out. I wanted him to try to understand others.

At some point Mr. Rhetoric interjected. I think he asked the child a question. The child was up to talking about how he didn't need school because he didn't plan on working, which Mr. Rhetoric wanted to know how he planned to make a living without working.

All this time Mr. Rhetoric had been pointing out vagrants we passed at every outing, and yet the child was looking him right in the eye, professing how he didn't want to finish school because he never planned to work. I think the child was talking about finding money like how the vagrants supposedly did it.

Clearly, right here the vagrant visual needed to be upgraded, or as I thought, the ends to Mr. Rhetoric's rhetoric weren't meeting. But Mr. Rhetoric walked right on by his own propaganda leading the child, with question after question, to shed every stitch of clothing he had on, off. A conversation or discussion that began with, 'I don't like how I'm being raised', leaped all the way over to 'I wished ya'll had never brought me those bunk-beds. I preferred to sleep on a cot, or on the floor!'

What?

Oh boy. Mr. Rhetoric really tried getting his arms around that child. Wow. Mr. Rhetoric fought so hard to lure his child on the other side of the fence. Why Mr. Rhetoric fought as hard as my sister who maintained excellent school grades, and always completed her chores, and who was only pleading to have her allowance raised. I can't deny though, that I wasn't in tears laughing after a whopping chunk of seconds behind my sister's last slice heard Mr. Rhetoric absolutely lose it.

Right here I'll drop you off, allowing you to pick your own visual of what rhetoric looks like turned inside out.

RHYTHM & BLUES

One day very recent my sister and I were joking about certain features I acquired that weren't exactly like the rest in the bunch. You know the bunch I'm referring to. It's the bunch with the cousin who ended up with the hazel eyes, when no one else in the family had hazel eyes; at least no one anyone could readily point at finger at.

This is what was sort of going on between my sister and I. We were trying to pair up my hair texture with a close family member. It was all in good humor though. We actually heard quite a lot about the relative I am supposed to resemble most in the hair and legs department.

But just to add sauce to the joke I teased I was probably the mailman's daughter, to which my sister immediately came off with, "Oh no! You are certainly Ronald Clarke's daughter!"

Yes I am. I am most certainly my father's child. Not only do we look quite similar, but we also share the same dry humor, and we think something alike. We look at life simply.

We draw a white and black line easily. It either is or it isn't. We don't spend much time trying to sugar coat things... well then again, maybe to some degree we do.

Sugar coating things is what gives writing its elasticity, not to mention makes writing a more enjoyable vocation, too. My father does the same with his artwork. I still haven't forgotten the cartoon sketch my sister was trying to illustrate, drawing the behind of a female digging in a bag for more food at a family picnic.

My father took the pencil from my sister to show her how to amplify the vision. When he was done, the sketch needed no commentary. The moon he diagramed hanging over an edge of a table let all that cast their eyes upon the drawing know once that woman came up out of that sac, the picnic was over. O-V-E-R!

I point all this out because although he and I rarely saw eye-to-eye, it in no way meant that I did not see myself in him. My father was the apple of my eye. He was my greatest mentor and teacher.

As a child, I awed over his wit and witty sense of humor. Before words could even get past his tongue, I was already doubled over. His facial expressions were just so darn funny.

Scramble up Woody Allen, Archie Bunker, Columbo, and Fred Sanford, and slide them all into a suit tailored strictly for Mr. Clarke, and that's my father—sharp as he wanted to be, easy to laugh at, and sometimes a long walk around a block to love.

Another motif he drummed up was this dry erase board, or for those politically challenged as we were, scratch the dry erase board and just call it a whiteboard. Now, before I get to stirring at the bottom of the pot, let me explain.

None of us were bad children. And neither was my father, nor my mother bad parents. We were, and I emphasize, a good family. But even so, he deemed it necessary to find ways to ensure we remained this way. He seemed drawn to inventing ways to keep us in line, for that one staid day in the future, when the last apple had fallen, and just in case I guess.

Just before the whiteboard came along he talked about how he had been practicing the art of studying our individual habits. Wait, hang on a minute; let me backslide some.

When we were young he used to test to see how much common sense we had by putting us on the bed to see what we would do when we reached the edge. It's called the visual cliff thingamajig, except he didn't use the glass.

My sister would crawl to the edge, stop, feel over the edge, and either stay put or turn around. My brother wouldn't budge. Perhaps it had something to do with him being the chunky butt. Of course I crawled over the edge. Regardless of how many times I fell off—nope—never saw a thing, which let my family tell it, I lacked common sense. But at least I have an excuse. I was born this way.

So, back to his claim of graphing and charting what we enjoyed most. Someway, somewhere he had been keeping tabs of our likes so that when we broke an infraction, he could levy what we valued most against us in the form of a punishment.

I guess the three of us learned early how to crawl into white spaces. White spaces are blank spaces no one sees until the space gets filled. We enjoyed our solitude just as much as we enjoyed playing outdoors with our friends. He had to chuck that gadget, along with the gremlin pulling up planks on a railroad. He had assigned us so many routine chores that there were no chores left to punish us with.

The last punishment up his sleeve however, was the one I like to think was his favorite—gnawing at us by waving the almighty dollar before our eyes—the whiteboard-whippersnapper.

This time he knew he had us cornered. In his amber at the pit of his stomach I could feel it cheery voice, he told us how money got everyone's attention. It's the same stuff I read about in a column where a sports journalist was getting Big Jim Brown's perspective on today's sports programs, particularly in the NFL arena.

I read over Jim's answers, which I must say, I was surprised with how intelligent and grounded Jim's answers were. And don't twist my words. It's not like I thought Jim rowed on the slow boat. It's just that as Jim so smartly stressed throughout his answers, today's athletes just weren't the first people to jump in front of with a pen and pad ready to take notes on something like... like discipline.

Jim sharing how unlikely it was steroids were being used from his view looking around locker rooms with all the injuries and benched ballplayers, really tickled me. I think that was the part in the Q&A where Jim didn't mind being quoted. He seemed quite resolute on that point. But Jim also shared something else. Jim spoke about discipline among today's athletes in a manner I rarely heard. I like to think Jim was talking about our whiteboard whippersnapper.

I can just imagine my father out shopping for that whiteboard. He was probably on a small budget, even though he went out and brought the biggest whiteboard he could find. Come to find out, he was planning some hellified tabulations. He was ready to really go to work on us.

But unbeknownst to him, this was to be his last trick.

He installed the one-panel wall-sized whiteboard in our TV room, or den, and then had us gather around to unveil his concoction. Oh, my father was way too excited as he explained the schematics of this whiteboard.

At the top of the whiteboard in a fat chiseled black dry erase marker he wrote each of our names. Me first, then my sister, and finally my brother. He drew a long line the width of the whiteboard beneath our names. He also drew more lines, creating columns for each of our names. You see, this ensured that no one got out of its lane.

The way the whiteboard worked was that each lane started off with five dollars. This was the amount of allowance we were allowed each week. Now mind you, my sister and I had to catch public transportation to and from school. Well, we could have walked the couple of miles except the *killer-K* was more convenient. It cost us two dollars a week for the luxury, which came right off the top of our meager five-dollar allowance. And I know. I know. Meager was a whole loaf of bread better than wheat flour and water baked at 350 degrees.

And yet still, whichever end of the equation this five-dollars got divided and rounded off, we rarely saw it. The five-dollars came and went so fast that the figure honestly looked better hallmarked on the whiteboard. At least that way there was some verification of where this money we were expected to create a savings from really went.

My father went on to explain the technical dynamics of his scheme. And yes, I call it a scheme because that's exactly what I thought the moment he started explaining, which is exactly how things turned out.

Every time one of us committed an infraction, he subtracted an arbitrary amount of money from our allowance.

For instance, my sister and I regularly passed our 2am weekend curfew. This was just an expected given since the clubs closed at 2am. I mean, anyone jumping up and down to lyrics where they don't give a hoot about roaches crawling on the wall, and the roof on fire, you know good and Bloody-Mary well have to close down the club.

I'm saying, we were in the club shoutin' about 'lettin' the motha—' burn down... with us in it! A far worse infraction would have been... GASP... being caught leaving the club early to mind a before the house burned down curfew.

Since that wasn't happening, our two-dollar tax infraction came right off the top. That tax infraction got tacked onto the other infractions that also could be infrared against us.

On a weekly basis we had the bathroom, the hall, the living room and dining room, and the kitchen detail. Usually the person with the kitchen detail could also expect to receive demerits, or tax infractions. Since the detail was a week long, it was easy to mess up one itty-bitty part of the tedious chore. All it took was one night missing to take out the garbage, or emptying the trash. Or maybe we hadn't mixed the toxins we concocted to clean the house with properly.

You see, back then we weren't buying things like Mr. Clorox bathroom disinfectants where ingredients like bleach, ammonia, and Pine sol were all mixed together. For the moment, forget costly. That would be far too convenient. Let my brother tell it, back in those days my father had us down in the cellar manufacturing our own chemical agents to clean the house with.

Let one of us mess up by not making the toxin strong enough to remove grease, or refreshing enough to smell like Mr. Clean. The cleaning detail cost us a many of infractions, like the one time one of us ended up leaving a mountain of greasy dishes draining. I think that was my brother because that infraction only cost fifty cents; the lowest demerit my father arbitrarily assigned.

Naturally, you might already see what ended up transpiring. Yes, my brother received very few infractions, while I racked up infractions. The subtractions going on beneath my name would make math a bad English joke. It was that ridiculous. I think my father was working on a second or third column for me. And mind you again, the whiteboard was one-panel wall-size grand, as well as he erased this board once a week. But when I say I didn't care, I really didn't care.

I stayed out well past curfew, even more consistently. I stayed in bed too late. And when I was out of bed, I wouldn't make it up. I cut up my box spring and stored my most precious writings and homemade paper-dolls in it. I missed polishing one of the living room tables; didn't Windex a mirror; refused to help my sister and brother hang Christmas lights; was caught talking on the phone past our week-day curfew; received the worst school grades... just on and on this list went—every week.

And I know. I know. Scratch the whiteboard and everybody watch this foot go to work. Well that may have chased away many of the infractions, but it wouldn't have cured the deep, dark, flat, don't care no more attitude.

And then, one day the expected unexpectedly finally happened. First, you must hear the whiteboard song my brother created. He created it just for our usual Saturday night shindigs—the nights when my sister and I had been out partying.

The song went: "We'd come home, slip the key in the lock, remove our shoes, and ease our way up to our bedroom. *Creak, creak, creak.* No matter how softly we tried to walk the floors always creaked, which my father happened to be a light sleeper. *Wink. Wink.* Sure enough, just as we had eased our way into bed, everyone in the house, regardless of how light or hard they slept, could hear my father moving out of bed... *eek, eek, eek*. He'd creep down the hallway towards the den, which for him it was *swish, swish, swish*. The light-switch in the den would flip on... *Click*... followed by the cap to the dry erase pen being removed... *Pop*. And finally, the scribbling on the whiteboard... *Screech. Screech. Screech.*"

The following morning my sister would hop out of bed and rush down the hall to check the score. Poor child. That whiteboard had her a jumpy, nervous wreck. Nearly everything made her a nervous wreck... well, everything except the sweatboxes where the likes of hoodlums with names like Chinamen were bouncing all around her. She wasn't a nervous wreck then. Maybe the music was too loud.

Any hoot, the next day my sister hopped right out of bed and, as usual, headed straight to the TV room. A few seconds later she was back in our bedroom demanding that I, too, look at the whiteboard. I didn't know what in the world new she wanted me to see. But I knew it had to be something unusual since she already knew how much I cared.

Sheepishly, but curiously, I laggard down the hall. Sure enough there was our customary two-dollar demerit for passing our curfew neatly scribbled on the board exactly where it was scribbled every week. But there was something else going on too. Apparently my brother purchased my father a birthday card, which my father tallied up two dollars to my brother's credit for having thought of him.

Oh my goodness! Can you imagine?

But you see, that two-dollars my brother received is definitely long gone. Neither one of the dollars probably lasted no more than a day, if that long. But what's the going rate for being well-disciplined?

CHAPTER THREE

"Rittenhouse Street"

The Meaning of Christmas

Where was my mother in all this? Well, for one, when her car was stolen she was illegally parked with the motor running and blinkers going since she planned to spend no more time inside the supermarket than it would take to slip thirty-five cents into a cigarette vending machine. She did get the pack of Tareynton's 100, but then a couple of guys got her car. That's just about where my mother was; if you get the point.

My mother flourished in a flaccid sanctuary that looked exactly like a flaccid sanctuary sounded. Like, a what in the world kind of peace.

She was the Tooth Fairy, Peter Cottontail, the Tiny, Tiny Woman with the tiny, tiny voice, the Little Engine that Could, the Goblin, and good God Almighty, least I leave off, she was Mrs. Claus, too.

She rose up like the Virgin Mary around Christmas time, which incidentally, was exactly when my father got to airing his concerns about another plot scheming to rip out another one of his pockets.

My father absolutely, unequivocally, before ever counting all of the reindeer it had taken to pull Santa's sleigh, hated Christmas. He needed to be incited no further by tying the birth of Jesus in with Christmas to know when a holiday had been overblown.

For every wreath that lined the streets, for every light that trimmed a house, for every commercial that offered another got-to-have-it gift, a new crease would show up somewhere on his face. By December 25th, he looked like a carbon copy of the Grinch himself.

But like it or not, he could huff and puff all he wanted. Like all the wind that wouldn't take down the three little pig's house made of brick, it wouldn't stop my mother from bringing Christmas to our home.

And no, she wasn't coming out of her pockets either. Remember? She flourished in that flaccid sanctuary. It was my father who she ascribed to tear out the hole in his pocket to play Santa—the same man who he vowed every day from the onset of Christmas what he would do if he ever got his hands around that fat-ass charlatan's neck.

But my mother could care less. For a good whole month prior to Christmas she wanted the house cleaned from top to bottom, and inside out. I can't recall for sure if she participated in any of this cleaning, but I know for a fact my siblings and I did, and so did my father. We cleaned the house from top to bottom, and inside out. My father supervised.

My mother also wanted Christmas lights strung up around the front porch, which again, I'm not so sure what percentage of her effort went into the actual labor of getting the lights strung up. I know my siblings and I participated in the hanging lights ordeal.

We had to select a color combination for the lights, and stand out in the cold to at least untangle and assist my father with getting up on a ladder to string up the lights. And there was more.

There was all the tree drama, which she again ascribed my father to take charge of. Not only did he have to buy the Christmas tree, but he also had to tie the tree to the hood of the car, drive a mile an hour through the city, untie the tree and lug it up thirteen steep steps getting it through the back door, and then drag it down thirteen steeper steps getting it to the cellar to soak in a tub of water. Don't ask why he didn't use the basement door. I think it may have had something to do with the thirteen locks we needed to secure the door.

His troubles were far from over. When it was time to stand the tree he had to shave the trunk to fit a tree-stand he also had to nail together, and drag it back up the thirteen steep steps; hammer the thorny piney thing into the stand... oops... where's the damn saw? The stump still wasn't even.

Say what you want but it sure looked like a lot of work to me, and one thing I hated was a lot of work. All the Santa and elfin drama made me think twice about the meaning of Christmas.

I promised I would never put my kids through all that trouble. My children were going to know the truth from the start. I wasn't going to have them showing up in the double digits arguing with their friends about whether Santa was real or not.

Do you realize my sister and I liked to have turned our neighbor's head around backwards for making fun of Santa? We were ten ...and eleven, I think!

To think my mother had us baking all those cookies for nothing. Talk about embarrassment. And that was just the tip of it. I wanted to know just who in a zirconium marathon ate all those damn cookies I had buttered up for Santa, anyway.

My mother claimed all this Santa stuff was good for us. Merry Christmas helped us dream she said. But I found myself asking if we were dreaming, or hallucinating. I knew of a much less labor intensive way to ensure a child dreamed. She didn't have to go through all of that trouble.

All she needed to do was let us hang around her best friend's children; the one's with the air conditioners in their homes, and built in swimming pools in their backyards, who wore new clothes at the start of summer and the first week of school, and went to the shore every weekend.

Just about when it got down to the tree trimming she shows up dressed in December's merriness, assisting with separating and repairing last year's tree trimmings.

The mangled and broken trimmings were tossed. The seriously old or troubled trimmings were put in a box and saved for possible use in another year. And the new trimmings got new ties and hooks for hanging.

Bows, and tissue paper, and scissors, and tape were everywhere. All that cleaning and the house looked worse than the day before it got good and cleaned. I didn't like it. I didn't like all the work involved. The monotonous work made the inside of my head itch.

I didn't care much about the extra stipend she sort of twisted my father's arm to make him give us either. The money did me no good if I had to spend it down to the last cent for somebody else's use.

Watching her close her eyes on all the preliminaries it

took to pull Christmas and Santa and each one of his elves out of linen closets, and cedar closets, and off tree lots and whatnot, to hear her keeping count of every red cent that came and went was too much. Way too much. Listen at her:

"Wait a minute! Wait a minute!" She always used her pointer finger for that part.

"Now the slippers cost $2.99. Your father's necktie cost $3.99. The play doe cost $.99 plus .03 cents tax. And the bracelets cost $1.99."

We knew exactly where she was headed, even if she didn't.

Sitting there looking over receipts as if she needed eyeglasses she persisted. "Now, if all this came to $9.99, and you started off with $20.35, you should have $10.36 left, not .04 cents!"

See, right there, the meaning of Christmas gone overboard.

On to track two she would want to know, and adamantly no less, where the $10.32 went. This drama happened to at least two of us twice. And our response was always the same:

"Well the $10.32 was for your gift."

Umm, umm, just like how I felt. Now what could I do with a gift that cost $10.32? Like I really needed to have to deal with another laborious chore.

Daddy Steppin' n Fletchin'

My mother's brother, a bit of a character in his own right, lived with us back in the day. This was back in the day when Richard Roundtree and other brothas' like him was saying things like 'give me five on the black-hand side', and 'so what it be jack', and 'cool mama'. This was back when black power fists, bell-bottoms, hip huggers, Afros, long side burns, and peace-symbols was on every other persons person; and places like Cuba and Vietnam was on every other third or fourth persons tongue.

Almost everyone was talking love and peace and war in one breath. Shows like Serpico was next to the coolest thing going, right behind JDs Revenge. And still, at least half of America—our one 'inth of a portion I know—was drawing energy off episodes like the Brady Bunch, and the Flinstones, Speed Racer, and the Munsters'.

This was a peace-loving time when neighbors were neighbors by definition, who even knew when uncles like my Uncle Red had moved in the neighborhood.

That's what everyone called my mother's brother—Red. That's because his redness really stood out. He was a big red man with big red hair. He also drove this big, loud, fire-red orange convertible Thunderbird. It was a sixty-something T-bird that came with an eight-track tape player to match his fly silk shirts and 200% polyester leg warmers. And not that my Uncle Red thought as much of himself as we, and almost everyone else did, especially the ladies, but he was one real cool cat. That's what men like him were called back then. Cool cats.

All I remember hearing was, "Is Red there? I saw Red here. I saw Red there. You know, Red looked good last night. Tell Red this, and tell Red that."

Red buzzed all around town zipping up and down the streets in his fire-red orange T-bird with the top down and music going, doing no less than the top speed a bird like that back then could do.

My Uncle Red and my father were two different people. Everybody probably could have guessed that, but what I mean is my Uncle Red had a great deal of respect for my father, even though people as straight-laced as my father weren't exactly his top choice for brotherhood. And then too, cool cats weren't flying around the top of my father's brotherhood list either.

Still, my father had a good deal of respect for my Uncle Red. I think they got along well because my uncle Red was so giving. He would do almost anything for anyone. When a sista' needed an escort to the prom, he was there. When someone's car needed a jump, or a spare part, he was there for the jump, and he was there with the spare part. And when we needed groceries off our short list... things like eggs, bread, and milk, he was there... like the day my father called over to the store he managed asking if he could stop by to pick up a half gallon of milk.

I can almost hear my Uncle Red. "Awl Ron man, we have plenty of milk in here. You don't have to ask, just come on by and get what you need."

That's exactly what my Uncle Red used to say to us; that being my siblings and I. When we came in the store he would tell us to get whatever we wanted. And we did. We would grab as much candy as we could eat before we got home, grinning all the way talking about how nice our Uncle Red was.

But on this particular day I heard from my mother, my father wasn't exactly grinning on his trip all the way home. And he wasn't skipping or walking his usual brisk-business pace either. But don't let me get ahead of the story.

As it happened to be, when my father got to the store he learned my Uncle Red had been out partying all night. My uncle's eyes were all red and puffy, which if my father saw anything red on my uncle, outside of his already whole red self, his eyes must have really been lit up.

Also, my uncle's shirt was good and wrinkled, which

everyone knows polyester fly-silk ain't so easy to get real wrinkled. My uncle had to have pressed the shirt while he was still in it sleep. He was lying on a counter full of bread too, and he couldn't stand up. He claimed his feet hurt too bad. He just looked overly spent, according to my father. He certainly didn't look to be in any kind of shape to manage a store for however many hours the store was supposed to be open.

But my Uncle Red was that kind of man. The storeowner wanted the store open seven days a week, which my uncle being like he was, was right where he promised to be seven days a week.

Because my uncle couldn't move, my father went on and got the milk and the other items on his short list himself. He even got the paper sack and brown-bagged his short list too. It was the least he could do, even if he was grumbling beneath his breath about how all that partying served my Uncle Red right.

Maybe this might teach my uncle a lesson about manning up to his responsibilities and joining the productive class of working folks. You know, my father was big on teaching lessons, even if he detested living by experience.

But as soon as my father reached the door my Uncle Red suddenly had a favor to ask. He wanted to trade shoes, which he really had to be desperate to look down at my father's Floreshiems and want to walk around in them all day.

Floreshiems didn't exactly go with orange hip-hugging bell-bottoms, no matter how extreme the flair on the bell.

But I can hear it now.

"All right Jerry." It was the least my father could do, especially with as pitiful as my uncle looked draped over a counter full of bread.

Just like that my uncle lost two inches—two whole inches he made up the difference for when he came up from beneath the counter holding a pair of two-inch metallic, sapphire I want to add, cycadelic platforms. That's what cool cats back then were wearing.

"Thanks Ron man. Thanks."

Now, let the picture be got. But what none of us could get was why my father, a man who sported much class and sophistication, would accept the shoes for trade, much less bend down and put them on—I think he had to lace up the shoes too—having everyone for several stretches of city blocks laughing at a mad daddy whose knees didn't ordinarily knock, bow out and buckle, stepping' and fletchin', and eventually crawling and grimacing all the way home.

GETTIN' THE BAD GUY

Fast thinking wasn't in the mix when Goshladang was stirring up my father. Goshladang had been doing a little too much thinking himself not to know that winding my father up as tight as he had him wound up would have him all festered in talking about what all was going on wrong in the world.

My father was always talking about what *they* should be doing and shouldn't be doing. It was always that proverbial *they*. But *they* never had a name. For all we knew, *they* was everybody but him.

Wouldn't it turn out to be that this one year would come gallivanting along when things at home wasn't all *they* could be. Although my father had been laid off a number of times, this particular lay-off seemed to have put us in a far more desperate situation.

The stews, and lima beans, and greens that usually got us through a few days at a time had reached the bottom of the last bowl. It was time to stretch out another meal—another meal that only pennies could work with. And who amongst us don't know that copper only stretches but so far.

Just before dinner my mother sent my father, along with my sister and I, to the grocery store to pick up that extra can of something we needed to expand our lean meal. I think our casserole was missing something like the tuna. Or maybe the pork-n-beans needed a can of spam. You know, spam and pork-n-beans went a long ways, too.

We got to the grocery store where my father headed, as instructed, straight to the can goods aisle, while I, as usual, moseyed around the front of the store. And no, I wasn't the lookout. I just knew my father was working with copper. I fully expected an in and out trip.

After a few minutes longer than what it should have taken him with only a handful of pennies to grab a can of whatever, I decided to investigate. I don't know what he was thinking, but when I peered down the aisle I personally thought he was leaning way too far over the can goods, studying them way too thoroughly.

I know he wasn't praying because I watched him pick up one can, inspect the top, and then place it back on the shelf. He picked up another can; same brand, looked at the top, and then placed that one too back on the shelf. He repeated this process a few times, which got me really curious.

The next thing I knew, he was down on his knees intensely and vigorously searching the cans. That's when I knew he had reached an all-time new low. Without a shred of doubt I knew what was coming next. I knew what was coming next because I had seen others up to no good striking the same deals—socks, and scarves, and nylons, and half of Woolworth's running up sleeves. Shoes jumping from high-end boxes to cost-saving boxes, and many other similar discounts.

But apparently my father had only heard about the discounts. Obviously, he hadn't seen discounts like the one long fingernail, two quick scoops and a flip; one in one direction, and the other on the can worked before. One, two, three, four real fast and *they* were out of there. Forget blink. Just think 'what...' and you would have missed it.

That trip really should have been an in and out trip.

Instinctively I looked around, immediately taking note that there were no customers in the aisle. In fact, there weren't many, if any customers in the store. It must have been an off payday week, or maybe everyone was as broke as we were. The store was so empty I can still remember the spit-shined linoleum floors not having one scuffmark on them. But no eyewitnesses' however, was a very bad thing. No eyewitnesses meant no diversions. He was out there on his own.

In absolute horror my sister and I watched my father down on his knees, with both elbows pointed toward the ever-glowing headlights in the ceiling, scrape a what? ...a fifty-something cents price sticker off a can of tuna... or was that spam? His all the way clean stubby fingernails were furiously going to work on the ends of a little piece of paper clutching at every corner to the top of a can.

Immediately we got to dialing up the Lord because we didn't think, or guess, or hope even, that he wouldn't be caught. We knew he would.

"Damn. Damn. Damn. Good Lord, please be home." We were a frantic, shivering mess. Everybody we knew who had gone down this way, hadn't been set up. They were in the state house for a reason, and we knew this.

But the good Lord wasn't answering. I was counting "1-Mississippi, 2-Mississippi…" He was just taking way too long to come to the phone.

"Damn it Daddy! Would you please get up off your freakin' knees before we all end up sitting next to your pals beneath cardboard boxes!"

Oh, just go ahead and already smack me in the face. Why was I even carrying on like this? Didn't I already see the end of our world, like yesterday?

Sure enough, a little intense clip-board grocer came strolling by the can goods aisle. Trust me, I saw the tip of the grocer's right shoe before I ever saw all of him. And I heard his thought before his eyes could register his complaint. I'm saying, the grocer didn't even have to do a double-take. He high-tailed it right on down the aisle just like 911, squealing and screeching, "Hey, you can't do that!"

Now this was back in the day when rarely did police show up in our neighborhood—thank every aspiring gospel of the truth. It had to be a triple something before the police would show up. A duo something, or definitely a solo anything, and you'd be looking at a good Samaritan as the police officer, and your ambulance too, if you needed one. The police just weren't called for things like fifty-something cents price swap-outs. Today however, break a fingernail flipping someone off and you get SWAT, Homeland Security, and CNN if you're real unlucky.

But we didn't need SWAT, or the police to feel threatened. The hysterical yelling the grocer emitted throughout the store echoed so loudly our heads rattled, our jaws shook, and our feet started going, moving as they were programmed by an alien force. Walk straight, turn left, and right here, STOP... at the register... and pay for the can of meat and get the h-e-double jell out of the store.

My father was scared too. He was ahead of us making it to the register, which I hoped like a praying mantis however many cents he was trying to scrap off that can, he had buried somewhere in his pocket. You see, there were no dishes in a grocery store to wash. A trip downtown was definitely the only option. And by the sirens going off in the grocer, it looked like that's exactly where we were headed.

The cashier, it turned out, knew all about the varied ways customers received those great sales and discounts. He acted as if that was the way his momma and grandmomma did all their shopping. He just looked over at the little clipboard grocer a whooping and a hollering, and making up all the racket, and nodded.

Whatever cents my father had scraped off the can, he promised the little clipboard grocer he would put right back on. Good Lord, we never thought we would catch our breath. But after all the *theys* my father regularly ranted and raved about, do you know what he had the nerve to turn around and say?

"See, the cashier didn't even care."

Was he kidding? At the very least, how about cross-referencing the fact that people were donating in droves at least two-cents a day to feed starving children in Africa.

THE BIG BLUE VALLEY

What line? Where's the line? Oh, you mean that line?

Yah right. As soon as our parents announced they were going out of town for a whole weekend, we knew we were stepping over that line. There was just no ifs, ands, or buts about it. We were going over.

The three of us, that would include my brother, my boyfriend, and me, moved towards the line by first trying to convince my sister to take a puff off a cigarette. We wanted to see her inhale one quick whiff, and then blow it out. It wasn't as if the cigarette was going to hurt her. Newport's were a top of the line brand. That is, they cost the most, which had to mean they were the safest.

But as close as we got, she couldn't and wouldn't take that drag. Man we were so close too, which this whole story might have ended right there had my sister taken that one itty-bitty puff. I might have one less story. Or maybe I would be telling one different story. Whatever story, maybe would definitely have been a different certainty had not my sister, being her same conscientious self, stuck to her guns.

Still, she was going over that line. We were sure of it.

That's how we fishtailed our way around to discussing buying beer. We figured if she wouldn't smoke, then maybe she might drink. None of us however, were anywhere near twenty-one. My brother was the youngest. He was about eleven or twelve. And none of us looked a day over ten or eleven. We all looked like babies.

Logically, this got us to discussing where we could buy this beer, along with settling appointments on which one of us would make the purchase. That's how the mention of an uncle who owned a bar in one of the neighboring neighborhoods came up. We thought it might be easier to convince a 'had to be cool' uncle to slip us a six-pack over the counter without the barrage of ridiculous questions.

I mean like, "Did we have ID?"

"Did we look like we had ID?"

"Hell no we didn't have ID!"

But we had ten dollars… ten dollars a cool uncle might see more of if he stuck with his role and stopped with the silly questions. Like Brotha' please, don't hold us back playing around with half a deck, wondering why we weren't using a full deck.

Settling the beer issue drove us directly to our next conquest. We started discussing how we would get over to the bar. See how these small-minded conversations flowed. No different from adult conversations. Just don't focus on the words. Instead, focus on the flow.

Having seen privileged television parents take these kinds of out town trips before, we knew exactly what to do. We did exactly what any privileged television child would do. We grabbed the car keys off the mantle and jumped in the Big Blue Valley—and hey, my sister too. Like I said, like it or not, she was going over that line. She was going right over, along with the rest of us.

We knew our parents wouldn't mind. Why else would they have left the keys out in plain view? That was how we explained it to my sister. The only hemming and hawing around taking the car keys was deciding who we should give them to.

Should we let my boyfriend drive, since he was the oldest? Or should my brother drive, since he could drive?

We selected my brother. He seemed more credible.

The weather was just right. With no more than a few scattered clouds, and blue steering ahead of us everywhere we looked, the Big Blue Valley with all four windows rolled down and taking its leisurely good ole' time, took us right on our way.

She was a pretty thing too. Her royal blue color with the long strip of metal running along her side let all those on the sidewalk know, we were riding in a Dodge Plymouth Fury II. Gotta add that II. A Dodge ain't nothing unless it's a Dodge twice the Fury.

Without a moment's hesitation, or hindsight reflection, my brother purged the Big Blue Valley on around a corner and hit a hill—incidentally, a hill in the direct exact opposite direction of the bar. No one said a word. Not even my sister who I could tell by the silent smile on her face, the girl was scared brain dead.

Truth be told however, all of us were scared. We knew what we were doing was wrong, but we ignored the obvious. The fact to the matter was my brother, reared way back and tucked in a corner of the driver's seat, had moved us beyond the parking space. The boy, barely even tall enough to see over the steering wheel, really could drive. That fact was no lie.

The Big Blue Valley smoothly navigated over a wide hill and then took a wide turn. We had taken on Washington Lane. Even back then we were amazed at it all. But looking back today on that day, I'd argue all the way to the National Convention, "that child handling the Fury the way he handled her was nothing short of a standing ovation."

Subtracting my brother's age, size, and on the road experience, all of which were a big clap in itself, the Big Blue Valley was a vehicle to be reckoned. She wasn't like some of our later more modern rides like Momma and Kerbeck, and Nellie even.

The Big Blue Valley had to be handled. When she needed to round a corner, you couldn't take a finger and wisp her around a corner. The Big Blue Valley took muscle and grease and know-how to turn. Depending on which corner you rounded, determined how much of each you'd need. Would you need muscles and might and a few choice words? Or how about just parking and taking the bus?

The Big Blue Valley wasn't no shot in the dark 'where did she go'. This girl was like a big blue valley—big, blue, and as far as the eye could take in, a valley. How in the world my pint-sized brother whipped her around a corner where the lane divider really meant something was a feat within itself. I take it back. This wasn't no standing ovation. The child was an over the top standing ovation.

Both my sister and I sat in the back seat braced like we were waiting on whiplash. Our eyes had to be as round as flying saucers as we watched in awe the Big Blue Valley making it down Stenton Avenue. Amazing.

I mean like, "Hey Seuss" I'm not talking about no empty dusty graveled up country roads. We lived in the third largest city in the country back then. We were right behind New York and Los Angeles. And in terms of landmass, we probably could sit inside both LA and New York a few times. And don't even let me get started with how many times Philly could sit inside cities in a state like Texas. What I'm saying here is you just don't go cruising down no narrow streets in a city of this size, in something like the Big Blue Valley. You just don't.

Going down Stenton Avenue was right about when the seriousness of our offense weighed in. Everything around us looked so personable. It almost felt as if the entire block of Stenton Avenue sat in one nine-by-twelve room. I didn't like it, which was also just about when one of us mentioned seeing the police.

Before my brother could even finish warning my sister and I not to turn around, both of our heads spun around 180 degrees—apiece—to confirm what we heard. Sure enough, approaching from behind was a big fat blue patty wagon. It was enough space in this patty wagon to cart all four of us off to wherever patty wagons carted children who knew better, but disobeyed their parents anyway.

Right on cue, I started humming the opening to that familiar old prayer.

"God please help us..."

I just wanted God to make the wagon go away. At first, it seemed as if my prayer worked. The wagon changed lanes, moving into the left lane. It wasn't exactly good, but according to the way I had known most wagons to pull over motorists, it was a whole heck of a lot better than it being right behind us.

The wagon pulled along side us, and then slowly passed. All the while my sister and I kept our eyes parked straight ahead. Now I'm not exactly sure how I caught all of this with my eyes stuck in one direction, but I did. I guess only my eyes sat fixed, while my pupils kept moving.

"Good," I sighed as the wagon passed by. The wagon was turning left. It had its blinker going and all. But man o man, just to think during all of that plotting and planning to jump on the biggest thrill ride, we hadn't thought about discussing bail money. I hoped to a heavenly baked ham we didn't have to start discussing it then either.

As the wagon inched ahead, so obviously turning left, we urged my brother to drive slowly. We didn't want him pulling alongside the wagon and having to stop, giving whoever was inside the wagon an all you want good look at us.

We wanted the wagon to go on about its business, because once the wagon turned, we planned to jump our tails back over that line and stay put. The thrill was definitely gone.

The light turned green and our lane started moving forward. The left lane had to wait. There was no green arrow giving them the right away to cut across traffic.

Thumpidy thump. Thumpidy thump.

I wished I could say it was the music. Unfortunately, or fortunately in this case, the Big Blue Valley's radio was on a permanent leave of absence. That Thumpidy thump, Thumpidy thump groove was only playing in each of our throats.

Either we could have raced on by, or eased on by. Either way we were going by the patty wagon. We eased on by.

"Good Lord! Jesus! Jesus! Jesus!" —the inside of my head ticking as we eased on by.

"JEEEEEESSSSSUUUUS!" —when the ticking stopped.

No sooner than all of the Big Blue Valley got by the wagon, was it when lights started flashing. A loud, short, dull siren followed the flashing lights. The siren sounded like the bell that used to go off in the schoolyard just before class started. That time we turned around. One of those Bonnie and Clyde-Elliot Ness turnarounds… 10-4 already transmitted.

The patty wagon indeed had gotten out of its lane and pulled directly behind us. So scratch the hoping to find an uncle that would sell us beer. Yeah, nix that. We hoped to find an uncle that would bail us out of jail. And oh, we were going to jail. We were so sure of it.

Both police officers stepped out of the wagon. One white and the other black. I'll never forget it. The white officer approached the driver side. The black officer approached the passenger side. The face of the black officer was my only hope the situation would not get out of hand. If nothing else, the black officer would know the difference between our innocent looking for a thrill faces, from the real stolen car deals.

The white officer walked up to the Big Blue Valley's driver side window and leaned over. Before the officer could get into that age-old familiar ID diatribe, my brother looked up and asked what the problem was. Both officers laughed. The white officer leaning into the driver side window and the black officer standing by the passenger door. The officers laughed pretty hard too.

"Step out of the car" was what followed. I can't even say that the white officer demanded, because he didn't. He just simply said, "Step out of the car."

But it didn't matter whether he shouted the order or fired off a round in the air. Too many times I had seen this scene played out. And all what I hadn't seen I had either heard or imagined. It took zero imagination to see what was coming next. We were scared, scared, plenty scared.

I wanted to jump out of the car and start running for help. But then wasn't this how all of the other incidents blew up? A frightened motorist hyped up by accounts he or she had never lived, only heard about, running like all the dickens from two cops with guns. Of course, he or she had to have done something to be running like that. You just don't jump up and start running without having done something.

I stayed put. Besides, where was I going to go running off too? You know, like get help from who? Instead, we sat in the car discussing that infamous one call and bail money, and how if those officers didn't beat the crap out of us, our parents sure as a Mary Poppins were.

We had an uncle already picked out and were dialing up every god and good Lord we could think of. Bacchus and Abalone, Hiatus and Hyena, Lucifer, Cupid, Hercules, Nagasaki and Hiroshima… we called them all. With three of us doing the calling, one of them gods was bound to answer.

I'ma go on and put it out there as I am sure by now many people in the black community recognize this. There are good cops and bad cops. Sometimes a good cop can make a bad judgment call. The police officers we encountered were officers communities expect and deserve. Now I wasn't thinking this at the time. But looking back, I always remembered that moment.

The officers told my brother to take the car home and

park it. If the car wasn't where it was supposed to be, they were arresting the whole lot of us, which the joy ride really should have ended there.

A few mornings later in the week—after all of us had wiped the sweat off our foreheads and buried the nightmare in beneath our pillows—that I got to open one eye to hear my sister clearing her conscience.

"What!" —my mother goes.

"I just had to tell you… just in case…"—that was you know who of course.

There were more angry-like words I couldn't make out, followed by my sister easing into our bedroom.

I sat up in bed. "You are so stupid. Why did you have to tell them!?!"

"Well… well… I didn't know. I thought maybe a letter or something would come in the mail and they would find out."

"That is so stupid! Why would *they* let us come all the way home and then send a—"

"—She did the right thing! She's supposed to let us know when things like that happen!" —I guess you know who that was too.

Rosemary

...And speaking of rides, let me get you on Rosemary.

Ok, so like I've been naming vehicles for a very long time. Let's see, I've got the Sparkler; a fitting name for a brand new shiny silver Dodge that hung around in its proper day and time. There was the Big Blue Valley; our fabulous furious Fury II. Momma was one of my favorites. She was my big black gal with the gold trim; my first luxury four-wheel drive. So you know that's a fitting name for a queen. Don't nobody top a list like ya' momma.

Nellie was the cutie. We talked to her as if she was a real person. "Nellie needs new shoes." When Nellie gets a little tired we pull her to the side of the road and let her catch her breath. Stuff like that.

Shoe Baby got named from her plate tags. The first three letters of her tags read: SHU. There also was Kerbeck and the Pimpmobile—my mother's fat caddies that loved to hug… and hog a road. I got their names straight from the dealership—F.C. Kerbeck.

And then there was Rosemary. I don't know why I feel like this bike should be called Rosemary, even though I didn't call her that back then. You don't even want to know what I called her back then. Today I just stick with Rosemary. Perhaps it was her golden hue. Or, it could have just been me taking up on an old custom. I always heard people referring to their modes of transportation as hers. It sounded more affectionate I guess. I just don't see toying around with a Bob, or a Fred, or a Murray, and hoping they would treat me with a like tenderness; even if Rosemary was made for a boy, and ended up behaving just like a man.

My father was responsible for bringing us Rosemary. I think someone gave the bike to him. Or maybe someone had it sitting out on the trash and he, thinking of us, picked it up. And not that he regularly sifted through people's trash and brought home the treasures, but from day one Rosemary truly was a piece of junk.

If memory serves me correctly, and I must tell you I have a pretty good memory, my father was through with buying us bicycles. Not including the tricycle my sister and I shared, he brought us each a bike apiece.

Oh no wait. He brought my brother two bikes. After someone took my brother's second bike off him, which was after my father told my brother not to take the bike to the park, my father called it quits on purchasing any more bikes. The first bike my brother had stolen he had left outside our garage, unattended and unchained.

So, the three of us ended up with the half ten-speed from a pile of trash, Rosemary. Now of course there really is no such thing as a five-speed-ten-speed bike. What I am saying here is that the bike once upon a time operated as a ten-speed. But something happened to half its speed. I don't know what. All I know is that half her speed was gone when we got her. You'd think that maybe if we had greased the chain a little more it would have picked up that speed?

Just about every other day something was wrong with Rosemary. One day her left lung was hissing out air. The next day it would be the other lung. One time she lost one of her shoes, which my brother—I think—replaced the lost shoe with one of his own shoes. Then her crutch broke off. He didn't bother to replace the crutch though. Rosemary really had no use for it anyway. Rosemary was perfectly fine lying on her side alongside the heap of debris we often parked her beside.

After a while I decided to leave Rosemary alone. I was tired of riding her and discovering something knew going on with her. She huffed and puffed too much for me. Besides that, she was a little embarrassing. Her squawking and squealing, announcing to our neighbors and friends she wasn't happy, got on my nerves. I got the point. She wanted to be left the hell alone.

And then here comes out of a clear jet blue day. I had nothing to do on this clear jet blue day. The room I shared with my sister was spic-and-span, spotless clean. My bed had even been made. I had the dinner in the oven, all ready to be warmed. And I had set the table. There was nothing left to do but take Rosemary around the block for a quick spin. That's all I was going to do; take Rosemary around the corner for just one short quick spin.

I dragged Rosemary out of the garage and walked her up our driveway. This was after having to go through the great exercise just to get her out of the garage. First I had to unlock the garage. Oh, no wait. First I had to find the key to unlock the garage. Then I had to move the pile of junk from around her. Old benches, and buckets, and tools, and rags, and crap we hadn't messed with in ages managed to continue working its way around Rosemary.

As I pulled Rosemary up she moaned and fussed a little, but then what else was knew. She always moaned and fussed when I touched her. I dragged her on out of the garage and up our driveway anyway. Fuss as she might, she was going for this one short spin around the corner.

I straddled Rosemary and immediately noticed her seat was twisted backwards. I spun the seat around and slapped her once—on the seat—to be sure she understood that's exactly how I wanted her seat to stay. Rosemary had some nerve acting all ornery. She had been built to ride, not lay on her side acting all mean and evil. The nerve of her.

I plunked my butt on her seat and started to peddle, but lost my footing. That was when I looked down and realized Rosemary was again missing a shoe. Oooh, Rosemary was such a pain in the rear. I peddled on anyway, minus the one shoe.

At takeoff there wasn't much peddling to be done. I was on the part of the street that sloped downward. We cruised on down the slight incline rounding the first corner with ease. The street on this part of rounding the block was flat, so there again wasn't much peddling needed.

With one foot peddling and the other foot resting somewhere near one of Rosemary's upper joints, I hardly thought about Rosemary's missing shoe... until I rounded the next corner. Mainly using one foot I had to put a whole lot of muscle into the one-foot peddling, the other-foot guiding her ankle uphill.

Get it; breezing downhill a short ways, then a stretch on flat ground sort of peddling, and uphill the other short way putting much effort into the one-foot peddling/other-foot guiding the ankle.

Rosemary rounded the next corner with the same ease as the flat portion of the other street. Peddling again was easy. We swiftly moved along. With a slight breeze shuffling past my face and combing through my hair felt like I was riding first-class on the Queen Mary with all the windows rolled down. Rosemary hadn't complained once. She had me beginning to think nice thoughts about her.

My short ride was almost over. Rosemary rounded the final corner that was to conclude her short spin around the block. Umm... I was satisfied.

Rounding the final corner Rosemary had picked up a little speed. Seemed like she was enjoying the ride as much as me. She was doing about ten miles per hour, maybe less, but not so much less. I calculated her speed by the number of inches my hair trailed behind as she whizzed on around that final corner. Just about then I needed to apply the brakes, which I applied. Well, I tried to apply.

I tried one brake, and then the other. Neither worked. I squoze and squoze on those damn brakes and not a darn thing happened. The only thing I knew for sure that was happening, and that was Rosemary had picked up a whole lot of speed. At this point I knew it was no use in pleading with her, since she didn't want me on her no way. I started cursing at her—loudly and vehemently.

Oh boy, that really didn't help.

Rosemary was like, "umm humm..."

I could see the heffa laughing and bawling her eyes out and all. She was having a good old ball racing downhill. Maybe I should have been calling her Bob, or Fred, or how about "you freakin' bastard!"

I stopped swearing and started praying. I got to praying that age-old familiar prayer tweaked just a little.

"Oh shit. Oh shit." That's exactly how I was praying.

At first I thought to let Rosemary do her thing and ride her all the way downhill until she ran out of breath. But it was a long way downhill. There was no telling what all trouble we would run into if I had allowed her to keep going. We would have been looking at going through major stop signs and all. I couldn't risk it. I had to come up with a better plan.

"Damn you Rosemary!"

I guess I hadn't finished swearing. It was all I could think to say as I leaned Rosemary to one side, toward the pavement, desperately putting my foot out trying to get her to stop that nonsense.

Oh boy!

The ankle from that one missing shoe caught the pavement before my foot. As soon as it did, Rosemary flipped up beneath me at the same time I fell on top of her center bar.

Did you know it is possible to see the erosion on the east side of Neptune from my backyard in Philadelphia?

Yeah, on the east side of Neptune there are these big reddish-purple indentations that looked they originate from claw markings made by someone really hurting, though more than likely, they were the corrosive markings of an alien voice screaming way too loudly.

Miraculously, some way, some how, I was able to stand and throw Rosemary from where I stood, in the direction of the garage. At that point, I could care less if someone made off with her. Whoever took her deserved her.

I struggled up the steps to my bedroom where my sister rolled around the bed laughing about the commotion she heard. Midway through her laugh however, she paused long enough to ask if I was okay.

Meekly I whispered I was okay, which was my sister's cue to howl like a saxophone butted off stage by a row of tambourines and one Mahalia Jackson with a lemon stuck in her throat.

Between the tears and howls my sister explained how my brother had removed the brakes to fix another issue going on with Rosemary.

Just flecking great, I thought.

I couldn't sit or walk for a month. So yes, you are damn skippy. I probably should have named Rosemary, Bob, or Fred, or… how about "you damn son of a bi---!?!"

Rosemary finally got her wish. I haven't seen or heard from the cow since.

Fat Cat

One of our favorite pets was our cat, Chang. We got Chang after spotting signs of a mouse being in the house. It therefore goes without saying; getting Chang was all my father's idea. And nope. There's no point even guessing. This story won't end up at your average run-of-the-mill tale either.

It was right around the Munich Olympics when my father first spewed, shaking like a leaf, "You see this? ...This is a mouse turd!"

We—my brother, my sister, my mother, and I all huddled around the turd not sure if my father was correct or incorrect. What looked like the tip of a chocolate chip morsel, my father actually said was a mouse turd. For a good portion of the day I know for sure, we had to listen to my father ranting and raving about this one mouse.

At first it was the cookout somebody had going on up at the park... you remember the one... the one last month where (and I won't include the word he used)... was spread out from one end of the park to the other. It was them! Those damn blankety-blanks lured that mouse to our house.

Then it was the government. The government was always up to something. If *they* weren't landscaping our skies trying to make the weather suit their tastes, then *they* were turning rodents into spies and sic'ing them into our house where I must say, quite a bit of mystery did reside within.

Next it was the poor man next door, God rest his soul for the man now is at peace, probably taking food up to his room and not cleaning up after himself.

But what can I say? My father ran the show. Knowing no better we had to take him at his word because for darn sure we had nothing to do with that mouse slipping in the house; not with the way we cleaned the house using q-tips, toothpicks, toothbrushes, and whatnot.

Helplessly bent on teaching important lessons, my father continued on his rampant rant. He pointed to a speck of a breadcrumb resting all alone on the countertop and educated us on the dietary regiments of mice.

Did you know mice can eat a speck of a breadcrumb and be full for a week? Or was that a month? For the rest of my days I will never forget how little mice needed to live on… for what was that? …forever? All of us will forever remember the subsequent run for our money this one mouse gave us—an ordeal that seemed to extend forever.

The never-ending forever mouse chase began with the attainment of our favorite pet. Now mind you too, my father had tried every trick in the Geneva book of mice preventions. Aside from the toothbrushes, q-tips, toothpicks, and concoctions and so forth, there also was the caulking. See mice could flatten themselves out and slip between amazing spaces.

My father caulked everything. The floorboards, doors, windows, ceilings, just everything. Our house was caulked so tight that during the summer it seemed easier to break the glass in the window rather than to struggle prying the window open.

But this wasn't no ordinary mouse. This mouse was on official business, sent to taunt my father; thus the purchase of a cat entered his mind.

For this one bad mouse that had outwitted him time and time again, he was hardly thinking about an ordinary house pet. All on his mind was finding one bad cat with the reputation his childhood alley cat, Mickey had.

Oh boy, Mickey had done it all. Mickey not only chased and caught all of the neighborhood rats and possums and ospreys in the area, but Mickey also provided protection for the family. And that wasn't all.

Mickey cleaned the backyard and helped move coal. He raked leaves, shoveled snow, and even did a couple of tree removals. Mickey was something. And get this... Mickey hadn't cost a dime. Not one red cent. Mickey just showed up one day strolling along a row of planks in the back alley, and pretty much took over from there.

With a cat like Mickey it's no wonder my father set his expectations for the cat he purchased to be at least forty times greater than Mickey. Chang was going to have to butter up his paws and do what no cat before him had ever done.

You should have seen my father purchasing Chang that day. He walked from cage to cage looking like a roaming wild animal himself. Closely monitoring the behavior of all the cats, and there were plenty in the kennel to inspect, he studied a cage full of Siamese kittens the longest.

You see, he had done his homework. After extensive research—umm… two to three hours' tops, he learned Siamese cats were the most aggressive animals among the feline line. So while we looked at the soft, furry, affable kittens, he tortured himself into a near comatose frenzy, demented on catching that one dang mouse. He had to get the smartest, most aggressive cat he could find.

And that's how he first spotted Chang; the meanest kitten among this one litter. Instantly I will agree, Chang stood out. He was a beautiful Siamese—black fur painting the mussel part of his face, fascinating royal blue eyes', black tipped ears; a chocolate point, I think the papers touted.

But right off the cuff, all of us saw the devil in Chang. It wasn't so much as his black tipped ears and the way he nipped and pawed at his siblings that tipped us off. It was his purr.

Generally, Siamese cats have a distinct purr; not the typical soft whiny tabby cat purr. A Siamese's purr is a long, drawn out, piercingly loud whine that sounds a lot like the actual word, "Meooooooow…" only without the M sound, and much, much louder. Chang had a meow to envy. He had the loudest voice box out of all the animals in the kennel.

We carried Chang home, mostly focusing on what my father said this cat would be able to do. He would provide protection for us. He would prepare his own meals, clean himself—his ears included, and empty his own liter box. That part we really liked. He would wax the floors, empty all the trash, hang Christmas lights, shovel snow, tar the roof, paint the moon, dim the sun… you know, do all the things and forty times more than what Mickey had done.

Sold.

Now, I sure to hate to keep doing this, but I have to take a step back. My father had no business buying that cat. I don't want to spoil the story, but unfortunately, no pet has ever faired well in nine-four-seven. And true too, this observation is all in hindsight.

But that's what I meant by our house being a mystery. I think it was something in the air. Stay too long in that house and you definitely start losing it. It may have started with our first dog—Tracy. It turned out that Tracy didn't like very many people. This wasn't an altogether bad thing since we had her to protect our house. We even tolerated her chewing up our stairs and some of our clothes hanging on the clothesline—see what I mean? ...Tracy was losing it. But then one day Tracy snapped at my father for disciplining my brother. Tracy had to go.

We even had a goldfish. To this day I don't know how... or why that goldfish did what it did, but it snapped out too. Someway, somehow the little orange critter jumped out of the fish bowl. Found it lying on the floor the next morning.

Least I digress... Chang—I think—means fierce in Chinese. We watched Chang become fiercer and bigger almost all in one day. One minute Chang was ripping and running around the house tearing up our furniture; swatting at our legs; walking around countertops and the table eating meat cooling off, bread, butter... just any and everything, and the next thing we know, he's weighing at least 20 pounds. I could swear it was much more, but I won't argue the point. All I know is that Chang turned into this fierce huge cat, substantiated by the silver-dollar size paw prints he left on our pitch-black linoleum counter tops.

I remember my father talking about putting Chang on a diet, when all we were feeding him were table-scraps. Well, then again, chicken necks, gizzards, kidneys, and kidney stones might not have done much for me, but it sure as heck did a lot for Chang. And don't mess around thinking Chang had a fat swaggering rear end either.

That cat was all cat. It wouldn't surprise me that my father hadn't turned Chang's papers over to finish reading the rest of his history; like him being part lynx and cheetah maybe. But I won't dilly-dab on that issue. We still had a mouse to catch. And my father, it almost appeared, had done his homework.

Chang leaped right off our countertops, to outright jumping on and attacking us. And please believe me, swatting and scratching at us was the least of our concerns. Chang liked to bite. Say what you want and believe what you will, but one nip is a gaffe. Twice it becomes a, "wait a minute now…" But when you see a cat with a face as large as Change's hunch his back, do that growl of a meow, and open his jaws… "I'm sorry… somebody go check that damn cat's papers."

It made no sense for my sister and me to walk around the house carrying a broom just to keep Chang from attacking us. And it was just plain plum ridiculous having to lock Chang in the cellar when guests were over; or keep him on a leash when he was outside. Have you ever seen a cat on a dog leash? Or better, have you ever seen a cat break a dog leash and take off after a dog; a dog five times his size? I use to could say, "I had never."

And still, we came to love Chang. His reckless personality grew on us easily. We trusted that if it was moving, he was going after it. Or if he could smell it, he was going to hunt it. And definitely, if he could see it, he was going to taunt it. Squirrels and birds, and other cats, and of course the dogs too, caught Chang's full bliss. There had never been so many dead birds lying around our house. No honestly... I really thought the air was coming down with a flu-like epidemic.

My father said Chang was a hunter, which was really nice to know, especially with all the mayhem he caused, and still not having caught that one dang mouse.

That mouse was behind the wall doing the cabbage patch and the foxtrot. Giving us the finger and flicking a few boogas at us. Rolling on its side and howling laughing for it had outwitted my father again. You know what I think? I think Chang and that mouse was in on it together.

Cross my heart, my hand held up to you-know-Who, my father had to get down on his hands and knees and catch that dang mouse his damn self.

JIM BEAM

There was the exacto knife accident. That was the night my mother got the call that sent her running off to the hospital where my father had been rushed to from work. Apparently he wasn't watching what he was doing, or was tired, sleepy, or all when he ended up resting his arm on an exacto knife he used to scale drawings.

There was the seamstress, when after my mother inquired further, realized the seamstress was just a woman who sewed a whole lot, and liked my father a whole lot as well.

There was the one gin too many. That was another night my mother had to go and fetch my father, from Broad and Olney, I think. That was a scary night. She hadn't too long ago gotten her driver's license. This made it about the second time she had been on the road. The first time she was on the road, we ended up lost trying to get to Cheltenham Mall.

These were just a few of the litany of tabletop work-related tales my father brought to the table. We enjoyed them all, such as the fender bender tale. That was the one place where my father was promised he could never work again. He said he wanted that promise in writing, in case the company changed names or forgot about him or something.

No story however, ever received more attention than Jim Beam. That wasn't the man's name, but it is a name that suits him to a tee. Jim Beam was our favorite. Nothing beats at the front of the store top shelf liquor when the dots just ain't connecting.

Jim Beam worked with my father at a publications firm some distance away from our home. That's what necessitated the carpool need, which good Lord, the stuff that poured out of that vehicle when my father got home, gave us all an up all night liver intoxicification hangover. We couldn't help but love some top shelf, Jim Beam. We must have sipped on Jim Beam for a whole year before we ran out of stock.

From point go, as soon as my father sat in Jim's car, with Jim clutching the steering wheel and staring out of lenses that looked to have been designed, cut, and stacked by Coca-Cola, he knew he was going to be carpooling with an exceptional driver. And I mean exceptional in a way that Jim Beam should have been the exception to all licensed drivers permitted to drive.

Barreling down highways, and parkways, and streets sideswiping trees and parked cars and whatnot, using the twisted reasoning such as if they can't see him, then how in the world did they expect him to see them is the special picture I'm drawing out here.

But my father rode out the odds of losing a limb, or worse, his life, because he was saving a hundred bucks a month. Are you kidding? A hundred bucks back then was a throw down Christmas, dinner and an allowance for a month, a week's worth of back to school clothes, and bragging chump change for the weekend.

Jim could have driven all 60-miles on nothing but pavement as far as my father was concerned. My father went on and took his chances snatching his arm away from the window and yelling every quarter of a mile or so, "Hey man! You see that!"

But of course Jim hadn't seen that. Jim was busy talking about, "Hey look man," that was the way Jim always started out, "you won't believe what happened to me last weekend."

My father never bothered to answer because he could believe it. Already only four of the thousands of tree limbs that leaped through the window, had narrowly missed him. And the door handle was still hanging onto the doorframe by half a screw. My father could believe it all right.

There was no doubt Jim had been moseying around, not even in the market for buying a 25-inch colored television, when his moseying around was obviously interrupted.

Who even cared why Jim had been out moseying around in the first place. Maybe he was out looking to purchase pinking shears, or maybe he had been counting parking meters. Whatever he was doing, one point was clear; two men riding in a pick-up truck, dressed in jeans, sweat tops, and wearing bandanas beneath their skullcaps had sidetracked him.

The sweat top, bandana wearing truckers had a brand new 25-inch colored console television they wanted to unload on Jim. My father could believe every word. He even could believe that Jim would look around and ask, "for how much?"

The truckers told Jim two-fifty, which Jim handed over two-fifty without hesitating. Two fifty was a steal for the 25-inch Panasonic colored television Jim described. Jim could expect to pay double for a brand new 25-inch colored console television that came in box with manufactured looking labels and staples plastered all around. Like what did my father know? He hadn't brought a new console anything ever. He was still picking up little portable 13-inch black & whites out of thrift shops and off pick-up trucks hauling trash to the dump. Jim could have paid $2.50 and my father would have still thought he was being taken.

Jim said he paid the guys in the sweats and jeans, who wore bandanas beneath their skullcaps, $250 for the television—the television inside the box with the manufactured looking staples and other labels all around. The bandana wearing skullcap guys helped Jim load the television into his car. It took four of them to lift the television. The television must have weighed a couple hundred pounds. At that point, Jim was done with moseying around. He drove straight home thinking all the way what he planned to do with his little 13-inch; the 13-inch with the hanger wedged in the port where the antenna was supposed to be.

My father didn't say a word. My father waited for Jim to get in the door, kick his little sorry 13-inch out the door, and open a box he couldn't believe only contained cinder blocks.

And then... and then, if not a day later, Jim goes again... "Hey Ron look man, now this you are not going to believe. I mean man, now this could happen to anyone..."

Once again Jim was moseying around a shopping center. That time Jim said he was looking to buy a pair of shoes. At the time, Jim was actually standing in front of a shoe store looking in a display window at shoes. A well-dressed man approached him. The man wore a suit, pinstripe I believe, and probably loud green alligator shoes and a pink polyester tie too. The man looked decent was how Jim described him.

The pinstriped man asked Jim which shoes he liked, which Jim pointed to the pair of skins in the showcase window he liked best. The pinstriped man was on it. He told Jim that he could get him two pairs of skins for the price of one. The pinstriped man was talking about giving Jim two pairs of shoes for only a hundred bucks. It all sounded pretty good to Jim. It must have. Jim took the pinstriped man up on the offer.

Jim shelled out the twenties and followed the pinstriped man's instructions. The pinstriped man needed a few minutes to get the shoes and then leave the shoes at the back of the store—outside a door… like outside on a back stoop or something. Jim gave the pinstriped man those few minutes and then made his way down the street and around a corner to pick up the shoes at the back of the store the pinstriped man had described.

The shoes weren't there. And neither was the pinstriped man. Jim couldn't even remember if a stoop was back there.

Save for staying on course with the story, Jim banged on the store's back door. Jim banged on a few more back doors too. When there was no answer from any of the back doors, Jim rushed back around to the front of the store. Yes, he sure did. Jim charged right into the shoe store and asked every salesman inside about the pinstriped man. And guess what?

No one inside the shoe store could believe it. Everyone stood there looking at Jim perplexed.

But wait... wait. There's another one... Actually there were many, many more. These are only the ones that come instantly to mind. They happened in rapid succession. Only Jim's bank statements might tell the rest of the mind-boggling, hair-raising story.

My father still wasn't missing any limbs when Jim got back to promising my father how he was yet another victim of what could happen to anyone.

Jim swore up and down that my father, too, could have been sitting on a bar stool working on his fourth or fifth shot of gin, with his back facing the door, obviously minding his business, when a man approached from behind and asked the time. That, Jim promised, could happen to anyone.

Never mind the medallion-sized grandfather clock that hung over nearly every bar in Center City. Like what man back then didn't rely on that clock for one reason or another? Jim instead went through the trouble of fumbling with his wrist to raise his sleeve anyway. The man, beaming wild-eyed, waited for him to finish fumbling with his sleeve before opening his coat and allowing Jim's eyes to feast on rows and rows of Rolexes pinned inside.

The man's coat must have been one of those Super-fly hustling numbers. You might recall the coat. It was the number all hustlers back in the seventies wore. Jim couldn't believe it. He bought two, got home, and after sobering up he rewound the watches.

Well I'll be a Sammy Watchamacallit if those watches didn't need a whole lot more than batteries to make them tick.

There was only one Jim Beam story we ended up not believing. Incidentally, it was the one story that cleaned off the top shelf.

Jim returned from a lunch break stopping by my father's desk to update him on their carpooling arrangements for the evening. Look out now!

Looking through Coco-cola lenses still in tact, but with a loosened necktie draped around his neck, Jim apologized for not being able to give my father a ride home, which—

—none of us, to include my father, could believe how Jim managed to be standing upright with his Coca-Cola's still intact, after wrapping his entire car around a three-hundred year old oak tree he swore hadn't been there the other day.

CHAPTER FOUR

"Venango Hall Leftovers"

Nobody's Food

After I got to assessing many of the stories that got the most air time around our table, I got to thinking how much I really loved my parents, my home, and this table. Someone, actually somebodies, occasionally asks, "What are you so angry about?"

I'm not angry. At least I don't feel angry, even if there are these bruised indents on my fingers, and despite having gone through a couple of keyboards. Maybe I just type angry. Or maybe by the time I get to the end of this book the love will show up because I know I say it all the time, over and over, I love my parents, I loved my home, and I love this table—the one element that has sustained us all.

But wow, right about now I have to admit even I sometimes look around and wonder, "where is the love?" And then what do I do? I go on to recall this incident.

Wasn't big as a minute, but I loved me some food, some good hot soul food too... and still do. I like to think I savor the flavors. Mayonnaise tastes nothing like Miracle Whip. Tuna is hardly tuna if it's not solid white. Whole vegetables like green peppers, onions, parsley, garlic, and celery seasons and tenderizes food better than any ground seasonings grinded up in jars. Oooo, let me stop here. The thought makes me hungry, which sometimes hunger has an ill affect on my temperament.

Don't know where all I ate went, tapeworms possibly, but I do remember loving some food. That's how I got to taking note on what was going on at everyone else's dinner table.

I used to watch the neighbors at the far end of the block. They mostly ate hot dogs and hamburgers. I guess it wasn't the easiest thing for the typical family that included two parents with professional careers, and a few children who moved between daycare, school, and after school activities to find time to cook a full course meal—a full course meal that included a meat, a starch, and a vegetable.

I guess you'd had to have an oven built into your briefcase, or backpack, to turn anything other than hot dogs and hamburgers into a full night's nutritional meal. And still, I salivated over those wieners and hamburgers, even if eating at various times and anywhere in the house seemed a little odd.

The neighbors in the center of the block I sort of liked the thing going on at their tables too. These neighbors in the center of the block consisted of two parents too, except only one worked. While the father was a politician, physician, or another sort of professional, the mother was the homemaker.

She cooked like I expected Opie's and the Beav's mother to cook—the pretty green string beans, nice fluffy white rice, and a tender piece of beef browned to perfection and always smelling as appetizing as it looked. Usually right around 6pm was when the father's car would pull up in the driveway. That's when I would get to see the pretty spread of stirring foods properly gracing the table, and be asked to go home. I hated that time.

The neighbors several blocks over, and around several corners too, I liked most. They had it going on. Chops, and beef, and fried chicken, and fish, and potato salad, and candied yams, and greens, and beans, and macaroni and cheese, and all the sweets and treats a child could dream up always sent my eyes rolling back in my head. Just one sniff and a good look made my ankles weak and my knees buckle. And get this. Both of the parents worked. They worked hard jobs too. And long hours. And still they always had enough for me.

Had not my parents taught me better, I would have been over to these neighbor's homes every day. I liked how they ate, even if they did sit wherever to eat and sometimes ate at odd times in the day.

So on to home I had to go. I had to go home to the table where either liver, meatloaf, eggplant, navy beans, beef stew, or casserole of some humble sort plagued the table. Okay, so sometimes there was chicken, fish, and greens. But those were rare occasions when my parents had gotten real fancy. Like where in place of water we'd sometimes have juice—orange, pineapple, or grapefruit juice.

Never ever was there soda or Kool-Aid. That stuff was supposed to be bad for our teeth, which to that end of a fully seeded advectionious sweet tooth, whatever beverage poured in our pint-sized glasses, we couldn't drink until we had finished eating everything on our plate.

We always ate together too. In fact, there was quite a bit of order going on at our table. The table had to be properly set, the food put in the proper dishes, and we always said grace. Not one day do I remember this order being mistreated. Not one day. Everyday it was the same thing. And if I knew better, it was the same meal too.

Okay. Okay. So trade the eggplant for squash, or

maybe throw out the casserole and replace it with asparagus. And not the pretty little asparagus tips either, which even those I'm not too sure I would have liked any better. But at least it wouldn't have been those robust looking spears that looked more like a branch of an uprooted tree. A kid's mouth can't even open that wide. Can it?

The point being, when it's neither hot dogs nor hamburgers, nor Opie's food or soul food, but rather nobody's food, it might as well be the same thing—nothing.

But you know what?

The order did us some kind of good. Good table manners carried us a long way in our careers, relationships with our mates, raising respectful children and so forth and so on. Had I not learned better, I never would have guessed how powerful such a small group words such as excuse me, and thank you, and please, and you're welcome were. And there was something else that took my siblings and I a long ways too. We didn't get to haggle much with weight issues either.

Well… okay, so I struggled the most with weight issues. But then again, look at who's hashing up all of this backwash recalling near fatal food strokes trying to exist off tapeworms creaming to lactose all the eggplant and liver I digested. You know, it is some kind of awful staring down six pork chops in the center of the table, hoping I could eat fast enough to win the tug-o-war over the remaining chop.

Ok, so now add chops to the liver list. But don't swallow a good thought. Aside from the fact that I can count using two fingers how many nights' chops were on the table, nobody's food had me weighing 100-pounds until I was twenty-six. By the time I turned thirty-six, I was still wearing size sixes, even though I was doing so a little extraneously.

I am now forty-five and comfortably fit into most single-digit clothes. My top however, is a little heavy. It takes quite a bit of muscle to push all of me into a single digit blouse. But all-in-all, I only have nobody's food to thank for being able to allow anyone who can get a finger in the back of my pants and flip it over, to see I am still wearing a size six down below.

All of this backdrop is important to letting go the account about this one New Year's Day dinner my mother swears never happened. But she should know better than to challenge someone who stared at a half-empty plate for sixteen-seventeen years, and rumored to be using a keyboard like a punching bag.

With how I love good hot food, I don't erroneously pull these types of stories out of my memory bank. Thirty years ago my mother really did get the grand idea to invite one of our first babysitters over for dinner. We hadn't seen our sitter in some time, which after learning about the birth of her first child with a fine man she had recently married, my mother decided all on her own to host a celebratory meal.

But as soon as my mother informed us of what she had in mind, I said to myself, "Oh boy."

As it happened to be, the last lavish dinner I had seen in our home showed up in a photo... oh... some many, many years ago. It's one of those pictures where I could be seen sitting in my grandfather's lap. Now that should be a good indication about how long ago I am talking.

But the spread going on at that table was some kind of spread. Before my mother even told me, I knew she had help. The pictures clued me in. In the center of the table sat a huge beautifully baked ham, flanked by a perfectly browned turkey just as large. And there were dishes and dishes galore of vegetables and baked goods twice as colorful and populating every remaining square inch of table space.

The vitality of the pixels in the picture really brought out the coloring of the food. I had never seen candied yams a more perfect touch of orange, or potatoes a more creamier fluffed up white, or green beans and greens and salads more greener. I wanted to eat the picture. And most definitely, every time I pulled up to the table and closed my eyes to bless the table, I prayed when I opened my eyes that heavenly baked pixilated picture would be there.

Point—blank, anything in the range of pretty edible and all the sweets you could dream up wasn't roaming anywhere near open flames in our home. Naturally, after hearing that real food was finally going to make its way near open flames in our home, it caused my ears to perk up, my eyes to look up, and my memory bank to open up. This I had to see.

Right on time at the appointed dinnertime our sitter, along with her husband and new infant daughter, showed up. For the first several minutes we cooed and awed over the baby's perfectly chocolate complexion, almost as if we were stalling.

People really do stall like this when dinner wasn't quite ready. But they usually did so camouflaged by at least one sinful o'derve tray. The golden dinner rule is that all guests arrive with a hefty appetite. They should expect to see some sort of food from the moment they step foot in the door. That's the dinner guest rule. It's the whole point of being invited to dinner. Like who wants to learn their guest, before arriving, dropped by IHOP and ate until they dropped.

In place of the o'derves, for guests who incidentally looked like the typical perfect guests, we took turns holding the baby, kissing the baby's plump cheeks, and counting all ten of her little fingers and toes. We asked questions like, how much the baby weighed at birth, and how much milk she drank, and then raved over her pretty brows, and clear eyes, and how much she resembled her father. And good Lord, we talked on and on about the baby's hair, for like a full thirty minutes or more.

The child really did have the thickest hair we had ever seen on a face as small. But then, there was only so much cooing and wooing that could be done, especially when it became evident by the spacing in conversation our guests were waiting to eat.

I guess I should have been thinking about dinner too. But I wasn't. Aside from being used to eating nobody's food, and nothing but pine sol and mop-n-glo smelling up our house, foods like lamb chops, and gravy, and mashed potatoes, and the kind of stuff that might make somebody wanna knock their momma out cold was the furthest thing from my senses. And then again, if I hadn't caught my mother earlier in the day stirring in the only vat on the stove I might have been looking for the beef too.

We pulled up to a beautifully set table, the one thing my mother insisted on getting right. She had the table etiquette thing marinated down to the red science in hot sauce. The fork and dinner napkin went on the left. The knife and glass went to the right. And the dinner plate went in the center. The salad fork, cup and saucer, and spoons we didn't need. Well, as it turned out, we really did need the spoons. I just don't think there were any set on the table.

While my parents drifted in and out of the kitchen bringing the rest of the this and the that to the table—you know, the butter dish, the salt and pepper shakers, and oh, the cornbread platter—I sat on the edge of my seat gingerly swinging my feet.

Sure I saw the vat on the table. I already knew all about its contents, but my parents were still making trips in and out of the kitchen. I think the cornbread needed a serving knife, and there was no ice for the Gingerale. Oh yes, we had Gingerale with our meal that day. Did you not hear? It was a special occasion. We had guests over for dinner—New Year's Day dinner, must I stress.

And then suddenly, like a chef left with the remaining task to turn out the light after the last customer, I heard my parent's sigh. They had spent all day toiling over dinner and now were ready to take their seats and dig in. Right there I knew. That's when I knew for sure we were in trouble. Our sitter and her husband, and myself as well, sat there looking at the table with the same plastic expression. "Is this it?"

Of course I should have known better, which brings me to why I didn't say something earlier. After my father quietly led us in prayer, and my mother commenced to moving a large spoon around the vat like a sad Tuesday in 1940, it dawned on me my mother really had not a clue. Clearly, she had forgotten. But I hadn't.

I watched our sitter part her lips, her best effort to mask a smile, and look down toward her plate. She wasn't passing her plate like everyone else. She just sat, as if she was sitting on her hands, and maybe swinging her feet too. No one, other than me and her husband even seemed to notice. Everyone else kept the plate passing flow moving around the steep silence like a hummingbird, stuffed and full, heading South. It was too late to remind my mother, but then whoever would prepare one dish anyway. Who?

I mean, go on and stick with tradition, but can't tradition be augmented for one special occasion. Must everyone be subjected to our stiff house rules? No slamming screen doors or closing room doors. No hip-hop music. No smoking. No drinking. Only straight, clean daffodil talking.

Finally, my mother sawed through the thick silence, "Lenora, aren't you eating?"

Lenora's husband answered, "Oh, Len doesn't eat black-eyed peas."

Ros-Poke

While I'm all wound-up, go on and add roast pork to the liver list. And while you are at it, go on and cross me off the truth index. I strive to tell whole the truth, and nothing but the truth, but then the itty-bitty unaccounted for facts always have a way of butting in, making me out to be a liar.

Surely by now, those reading the fine print, and the print between the fine print, can clearly see I am up to using my toes to finish this count.

Yes indeed, one Sunday my mother actually roasted a side of pork that nudged my pituitary glands to swell. All kidding aside, this Sunday we had roast pork, baked potatoes, green beans, gravy, and what the heck, I'm in a good mood. I'ma even throw in cranberry juice to rinse it all down.

I was a finger licking fool that Sunday. I mean, I ate and I ate, and I ate. We all ate. And after our stomachs stretched to a point of no return, there still was enough roast pork leftover to pick up from where we left off the following day. So there. That's the whole truth, and nothing but the whole truth. But, I bet no one would ever believe that by day two, that roast pork cooked to perfection, was the same roast pork to be out done by Pepto-Bismol. It might be a whole lot to swallow at this point, but please believe me when I say that this is not a flibbing trick…

…like the flibbing trick my brother pulled on me one day. That boy had me studying him like a hawk waiting for him to smoke a cigarette—the butt and all—until it was no more. He smoked the cigarette until it was no more all right. When the cigarette got down toward the butt, my brother flipped the butt into the street, brushed his hands together and said, "See, no more."

Now see, that was a flibbing trick. Pepto-Bismol beating out our pork roast however, was not. With the way lip-licking meals tippy-toed its way in and out of our house, it can pretty much be ruled out, we hadn't ever flipped a side of anything as good going down as that roast out in the street.

What flipping had happened was, I thought my brother had for once in his life gone out of his way to do something nice for me. The night after our big fancy meal it was my turn to set the table and reheat the leftovers; the finger licking good leftovers.

It had to be the nicest surprise to come home and find our meal already ready for reheating. Since my sister wasn't home, I naturally assumed my brother had taken the food out of the refrigerator and put it in the oven for reheating. All I had to do was turn the oven on and set the table.

Oops. I forgot one major detail. When I walked in the door after getting home from school, I met a stench like never before. I asked my brother about the odor, which he shrugged me off, leaving me wanting to tell him off about his funky feet, save for the nice thing I thought he had done for me. When my sister came home, the first thing she too harped on, was the funky scent. I told her my thoughts, which she too shrugged and moved on. I had no other choice. I worked around the funk, continuing with the kitchen detail until my parent's arrived home.

Now my parents were quite a bit more concerned. They had an investment to look after. When things went wrong, they had to pay. And something was definitely wrong. Naturally, they would be more concerned about finding the source of this very definite unidentifiable wrong, which by the time they arrived home, that very unidentifiable wrong was still lofting in the air.

I recall my mother checking the cabinets, and the refrigerator, and the trashcan. My father checked those place too, especially the trashcan. They wanted to know what in the heck had possibly died and taken a rain check on going to heaven. But neither my father, nor my mother could find what was so wrong. They had no other choice but to hope and wait on the wrong to get right; like we did that time my mother had picked up those two-for-a-dollar sneakers my brother wore until the soles passed out. That's what made us so suspicious of my brother; remembering his funky Woolworth's clearance sneaks and taking note of his obvious lack of concern.

We sat down as we customarily did, bowed our heads and said grace. Quietly we passed around the dishes. Nothing on the table was out of place. The food was all there just like the other day. And it tasted much like it had the other day, too.

But dang, something still wasn't quite right. Just in case, we sniffed over our food and took careful bites—again, just in case. Nothing seemed amiss so we went on started chomping down while one by one, with the exception of my brother, we relived how we came to meet the funk.

I rehashed how I found the odor when I got home, and where I thought the smell smelled the strongest. My sister added her two cents, followed my father asking a barrage of questions. Apparently none the discussion was sitting right with him.

Regardless of who smelled what first, and where and when, my father had one concern. Where in a suffocating breeze was the sinful smell coming from. And if there was one thing we knew best about him, and that was his love for playing detective. Instantly we knew what he was thinking. He smelled a rat, which if there was another thing he hated more than a scheming mouse, and that was a low down rotten rat. If the source of the smell wasn't isolated soon, every wall in our home was coming down, and he was starting the project immediately after dinner.

Before my father could leave the table for his tool bag, my mother asked how long I warmed the meat. Apparently, it wasn't necessary to reheat pork for a great length of time. I told her I hadn't reheated the meal for an unordinary amount of time—20 to 30 minutes tops.

My father, however, wasn't satisfied. He wanted to know when I had taken the meat out of the refrigerator to reheat. Now all of this discussion was taking place as we were blithely lifting our forks to our mouths and chewing fantastic portions of every dip.

All perky and real happy like, still charmed by believing that my brother had helped me out, even though I hadn't thought to thank him, I went on to explain how the roast was already in the oven when I came home—thanks to my brother.

People. People. I urge you to take heed. There is nothing paranormal about gurgling curdling animal protein. There however, is all kind of magic factored in Pepto-Bismol.

Let's see, it is sweet and a little smooth on the tongue, something like a strawberry milkshake. And it is heavy enough to coat your stomach and fill you up for one night.

CHAPTER FIVE

"Center City Attractions"

THE BLACK MAN

The Black Man couldn't tell one story that wouldn't take a turn at the first corner and run straight down hill a couple of hundred years.

Kicking up dust as he went, this man would race downhill snatching up all the anarchy and rebellion, and heroism and Robinhoodnism he could hold onto as he went. And when he got to the bottom of the hill, knees scaly and scarred, and straw and corn husk clipped to the ends of his hair, it would be Paul Revere and the world Paul Revere lived in that inevitably had cushioned his fall.

Sweeping up more mess than a modern day Shakespeare was how this man rounded up most of his stories. And still, no matter how annoyed or troubled his family was by the long feral accounts, everyone in his wake enjoyed the anecdotes.

It's like that thing he had against Christmas. Now his family thought they knew in and out why he disliked Christmas. Anyone who hasn't skipped any pages in this book would have a pretty good idea why the man disliked Christmas, even if it had come out of one point of view. The smart ones really do know how to read between the lines. Well, read between this line...

One year like last year this man had his family gathered around explaining why he disliked Christmas. Come to find out his hate stemmed from a year when he had run out of the house at the last minute buying gift-wrapping paper.

Whaaaddd??? Had the family heard him right? Did he say run?

That man, as far as they knew, never ran out of the house for anything. The only place he'd ever been known to run was around a track field... or when he was running someone down; like the afternoon he was running down those thieves cruising along Broad Street in his Rambler.

Other than that, that man slowed way down when the need to run necessitated actually running. And you can bet every day that has already passed, he definitely hadn't run after anything wrapped in Christmas. But the story gets better.

The Black Man insisted he zipped into a store where the sales people all jumped upon his entrance. Three white women, and one white sales manager. Although he hadn't added this part to the story, but the sales manager probably wore his sleeves rolled up, and had a pencil behind one ear. He probably had just finished inventory and was jostling with his favorite gals before calling it a night; when lo and behold good Lord look at what walked in—nothing but trouble.

The sales manager, sleeves rolled up and one pencil behind his ear, according to the Black Man, held the women back. With his arms spread out eagle style and backed against three frightened white women, the sales manager promised he would handle any trouble—particularly the elderly partially balding Black Man wearing the threatening eyeglasses and chimney colored jogging suit two sizes too small.

Flashback! Flashback! Roll every tape back and there almost always was that one defining moment outlining the outcome of an error taking a wrong left turn. This was the Black Man's error defining moment.

The Black Man said he stood there, conveniently observing all of this. But instead of leaving the store, he decided in all the infinite wisdom of intelligence, and in honor of upholding the one holiday he hated most, to allow the store manager to handle him by offering to take him out back.

Out back?

They knew the story was going to be good. The story could only get better since it had so much room to grow. The Black Man, of all people, had to know what being invited out back meant.

According to his testimony, and doggonnit he should know since he was there, the store manager said there was a warehouse out back—like a warehouse that held all the wrapping paper one black man could carry out of a store without bothering to stop at the register and pay for it.

It was time to check the man's forehead. He had to be running a fever. He could have been burning up with fever and no one had known it because no one bothered to check. No one could make up this story and not be sick. Who was he kidding?

Whenever or wherever in Philadelphia, America was there ever a warehouse behind a store? Come on now Mr. Black Man. Wal-Mart, K-Mart, Rite-Aid, gee-whiz… even the Sunoco gas station were right in the neighborhood. There were no warehouses behind those storefronts.

Had the Black Man forgotten 1600-something had already past? Was his calendar flipped to the wrong page? Just where in the 2000-something was the Black Man?

Maybe he meant 'in the back', which even that didn't explain the courtesy phone. That was the phone just beneath the blue light. Had he bothered to pick it up he would have found it worked almost like the phone everyone on the block used back in his day.

Oh well.

But now, everyone remembers Cujo right? —The rabid dog that terrorized a small Midwestern-looking community. Well Cujo was in the warehouse, so said the Black Man—Cujo and all the wrapping paper one elderly, partially balding, threatening eyeglasses Black Man wearing a chimney colored jogging suit two sizes too small could carry out of the store without stopping by the register to pay for it.

Right there the family was done. Marinated, seasoned, flipped over, cooked, turn the oven off and stick a fork in each one of them; they were done.

Did the Black Man ever purchase the gift-wrapping paper? Maybe, or maybe not. Whose gifts did he end up wrapping? Nobody knows. Did Cujo get fed that night? Most likely so. And did the family believe the story? Heck no! The only thing they knew for sure, the Black Man has never liked Christmas since, according to him.

CAROLE BRADY

No, not Weezie, or Florence the maid, or Esther Rolle even, but Carole Brady of all ironies was the Black Man's wife. Of all men, what was the Black Man doing with a woman who upheld the ideal dream of the American woman? Cleopatra, Queen Nefertari, or Yaa Yaa (Asantewa) even. Anybody but Carole Brady. Goodness, anyway the Black Man tried, his story was just going to get knottier and knottier. For cripes sake he actually said I do to a woman who fulfilled every ideal of what being the accepted mother in American meant.

Carole was the pampering type. She smiled, never yelled, rarely raised her voice, looked up to her husband, and always pampered and fussed over her children. She did, however, smoke those squares. But she smoked the minty dainty squares she could line up in fancy cigarette cases. Back then who was telling? Off camera, Carol probably smoked too. A lot of women did. It was chic in those days.

Otherwise she didn't drink, swear, or run the streets. The Black Man had him a real refined woman. Carole was a real mild-mannered lady who Early and her siblings skipped over when it got down to telling the parent most likely concerned about an incident where a teacher went overboard.

As Early described the spitting incident, she really thought she was only talking to the Black Man. Carole hadn't turned around once. Carole kept her eyes parked right on page 199 in one of Penny Press's best fill-in puzzles.

So what if the teacher flunked the student's presentation because he had a rag hanging out of his back pocket. And so what if the student objected to his failing presentation grade by walking over to the teacher's desk, politely touching the teacher on the shoulder, and begging the teacher to give him another chance. So what.

Carole wasn't listening. Carole hadn't paid Early one iota of attention. She didn't even budge when Early described how her teacher snidely turned around, gathered a hawk of spit, and spat on the student's hand.

Carole acted like she could care less. Her forte was in baking cookies and hiding Easter eggs; eating snickers bars, following the law; and you know, working those crossword puzzles and stuff like that. Carole didn't mess around with things her husband, the Black Man, was best suited to handle. Early might as well have leaned over and told her 6-across was Redford, as in Robert Redford.

Another week went by before the spitting incident resurfaced. It was the day after a parent-teacher conference.

Like always, only the Black Man and Carole attended the conference. Early never attended the confession sessions. She never had been invited, not that she would have accepted the invitation had it been extended. She hardly wanted to be in the proximity of the Black Man's reach should one of her teacher's decide to turn the tables on her. Early stayed home.

The Black Man and Carole returned home from the parent-teacher conference strolling right on by Early's room. Neither one of them said one word. That was odd, Early thought. Was she doing well in school or what? Never mind. No need in pressing the issue.

Early walked into the classroom the following day, buzzing up some real mess about Carole. Borax wouldn't have washed out the words her classmates put in Carole's mouth. Early's classmates were saying things about Carole she had no doubt was an embellishment to the highest degree. Carole never talked like that. The only four-letter words Carole used spelled words like love, and give, and play nice.

But her classmates were adamant. No, it was Carole who had used the filthy language. They weren't mistaken. They had watched the entire profanity beat down. Carole, shimmering in her golden locks and blue eye shadow, had connected at every stanza.

Rows and rows of lamentable words all stuck together. No other words got in. The conference lasted an hour. It was supposed to have been fifteen to twenty minutes, but Carole had a lot to say. Carole was a bad b-i-t-c-h. She had won the beat down. Early should have been there. She missed it. Could they borrow Carole's profanity book?

Had those foul-mouthed kids lost their minds? They were making stuff up and that's all there was to it. They were putting words in Carole's mouth, Carole Brady herself wouldn't have used, even if the director himself had promised to write her out of the script if she didn't.

Early dismissed her classmates. They had the wrong vulgar mouth parent. Obviously someone's parent had set the teacher straight, but it wasn't Carole. Early was sure of it.

Early went straight home and told Carole what her insolent classmates had to say about the uncouth parent who they claimed was Carole. She went from A through Z listing all the words in the profanity book her classmates had asked to borrow. 'Half of the shit, most of the shit, all of the shit'… She zipped through every piece of shit her classmates claimed Carole said.

Early waited on Carole's response. Early waited and waited. Knowing nothing about body language, Early figured Carole's looking down had something to do with her sophisticated emoticons. That's how Carole was. She never showed out.

Early sort of twisted her head one way sideways, and

then the other way sideways. It took a while, something like thirty years before Early, and all of Early's first, second, and third cousins got to see with their own eyes the inside of Carole's mouth. No one could believe it—aunts, uncles, grandkids, neighbors peeking in. No one.

Carole couldn't be called Carole after that. Beneath the golden locks and blue eye shadow really was Cleopatra the revolutionist after all. Poor Black Man. No matter which way things went, he wasn't catching a break no way, no how. He got his Yaa Yaa after all.

A Hooligan, A Painted Cat & Humpty

What did they want?

Education.

...and when did they want it?

Right now!

The Black Man and his wife Carole, when she actually was Carole, kept telling their children once all the meeting and discussing, and political crusading and educationalism got squared away, one day in the future was going to scoop them up and shoot them over a prodigious horizon.

According to the Black Man and Carole, one day in the future held one panoramic view. Whooping Cranes, Snow Owls and Flamingos beneath Neptune skies, overseeing Zimbabwe grass, money growing on trees, with pests minding their business, amid a Mediterranean climate where all meetings started on time and ended on time was the panoramic view smart people were talking about. Wasn't going to be another tear of despair in the sky once all the meetings and crusading got over and done with.

How lucky Early and her siblings had to be to have two smart parents. That's what everyone kept saying, "Wow, how lucky they were." At a time when other children were allowed to waste time having fun being children, Early's parents were teaching them about Snow Cranes and Zimbabwe skies and what not. They sure were ahead of the bunch.

But what Early and her siblings really wanted to know was, if their parents knew all the in's and out's of all this political crusading, and activism, and educationalism, and had their eyes good and parked on that subliminal one day in the future, then why in all of the Dred Scott decisions did they not know that all the children in the neighborhood were going treat-or-treating on Monday, October 31, instead of Sunday, October 30?

The Black Man and Carole insisted up and down, in and out, it didn't make sense to celebrate Halloween on a

Monday, when Sunday was more convenient. But Early and her siblings were thinking, just who were they to redirect what kid's holiday made sense.

Halloween wasn't politics. And Halloween wasn't anything to get an activist group going on and on about either. Halloween was just a fun night out where children dressed up, got lots of candy, and had a boat load of fun wondering who was what, and who got what. Maybe one day in the future Halloween might be celebrated the way they thought it made sense, but until Halloween light years away from one day in the future got where it was supposed to be, Halloween was gettin' celebrated on Monday, and not Sunday.

If only Early and her siblings could have convinced the Black Man and Carole. But they couldn't. At least not before the Black Man and Carole sent them off trick-or-treating on Sunday, October 30.

Little Sunday dressed as a bum.

It hadn't taken a whole lot to dress Sunday. He already had the stroll and the shifty look just right. All he needed was to grab an old shirt and pair of slacks from the Black Man's closet. Slap one of the Black Man's old Stetsons on his head, along with wrapping any one of the Black Man's cherry ties around his neck, and whaala… there was your bum.

Early went as a prostitute.

Go figure, or rather good grief. Could the child have

not come up with anything better? On second thought, leave that answer alone. But here's a tip for all you procrastinators with a lot of night walking work to do. Get a pair of stilettos that look just as good around your wrist as they do on your feet. And while you are at it, you might want to sew in your wig if you decide to wear one. And hey, spandex is a trademark of the trade for a good painted cat reason.

Nervous wreck tipping on nails was the fat man.

Nervous wreck was as bad off as Early, only worse. At least a prostitute could peel off the extra crap she didn't want to have to deal with going up and down flights of steps for nothing. The wig, the heels, the loaded earrings and jewelry easily fit in her trick-or-treat bag. It wasn't like there was anything else going in there.

But poor little nervous wreck tipping on nails in the fat man's fat was padlocked in her Halloween fat. Even if she loosened her belt and lost the padding, she had better not return home without Carole's good pillows. Nervous wreck tipping on nails had to carry those bad boys.

Climbing up and down planks of steps in the dark, with their Uncle Red who seemed as annoyed as the three of them, every so often telling them to hurry up, made them out to be the neighborhood hooligan, painted cat, and humpty joke.

One neighbor felt so sorry for them that she went in her kitchen and fixed them a warm snack. Hot cocoa, muffins, and stuff they had to sit at a table and eat. With the exception of Uncle Red, no one wanted to get up from the table. They dreaded counting the squares of paved sidewalk that stood between them and getting home.

So, what did Early and her siblings want?

Now-n-Laters, Blow-pops and M&Ms; both the plain and peanut kind.

...and when did they want it?

Monday, October 31!

SUE-ELLEN

I sure hope Sue-Ellen doesn't get offended. But if it's any consolation Sue-Ellen, they call me crazy, too. Like you, I see what I am not supposed to see, and talk about it.

When I see someone who waited too long to get married, getting married, instead of joining the huddle to whisper along with everyone who is thinking it, I let it be known; "Hey, that sure was one crazy wedding."

When I hear someone talking about a long-distance relationship, instead of joining the huddle discussing behind this person's back how fast downhill the relationship might go,

I don't hesitate to say out loud, "I don't know when I have ever seen a long-distance relationship pan out."

Sue-Ellen, you know how much I really hated seeing that young woman run out of the office bawling her eyes out. But I haven't seen a long-distance relationship pan out. It didn't mean the relationship wouldn't work—which incidentally it didn't, it just meant I never saw one work. Sue-Ellen I hope you know how absolutely horrible I felt.

So Sue-Ellen, I apologize. Two words I know you are quite familiar with.

I know how it feels to have a sister praying all the time I would pick up some cool points and keep a friend longer than a minute. I know how it feels to have so much to say at tea parties, and networking galas, and Christmas parties, and team meetings for goodness sake, but instead I have to bite my tongue to keep from saying the wrong thing. Instead of picking up cool points and friends, I usually end up being tagged aloof, and goofy, and odd, and all other sorts of off brand names.

Honestly Sue-Ellen, aside from being tagged many unpleasant names, most of my problem was not keeping up with good friends. Despite what they say, we have plenty of enough good friends. Real friends. That's because we know when someone really wants to be our friend.

We happen to know hanging out at our house, drinking up all of our liquor, and laughing at half our jokes is not what real friendship is all about. Especially not when come Monday morning we call crying to our supposedly good friend about getting fired, and this supposedly best friend cheers us on with, "Hey cool! Me too!"

Sue-Ellen we know that while misery may love company, this is just not our brand of friendship.

It's like the other day, just recently. I was getting my eyes examined because I am getting old and can't see. During the exam the doctor drummed up small-talk to, I guess, show me how friendly she was. Sue-Ellen, I think the doctor believed I would think she was my friend.

But you see, like you, I also have this sixth sense of knowing when someone has no intentions on really being my friend. And yes, we are not clairvoyant. It's just difficult to miss someone admiring my pink suede slip-on loafers, and asking if they kept my feet warm and whether or not they were comfortable, and know they weren't being sincere.

Now Sue-Ellen, you and I know what everyone else is thinking. What's wrong with admiring my pink suede slip-ons?

Well let's tell them what's wrong with that.

Before I even got to answer the doctor, I knew the woman didn't like my shoes. I knew the woman didn't like my shoes because who in a strawberry mansion wears shoes that are both uncomfortable and not warm… and Sue-Ellen come on now, and be pink, too?

Sue-Ellen, really? Whenever have we ever heard someone admitting his or her pink, obviously fashionable Van Eli's, were not comfortable? Not only did this woman not like my shoes, but she also was making me out to be a fool, a character we are sick and tired of being pegged to play.

Sue-Ellen, I told the woman my shoes were indeed both warm and comfortable, and I wore the shoes whenever I had to take long walks... like that day. But Sue-Ellen, do you know what the forthcoming doctor, who incidentally acted like she wanted to be my friend said in response to me?

Sue-Ellen the doctor said, "Oh, I wear my sneaks when I know I have to walk!"

Can you believe the doctor actually said that?

Now I know I have stretched and stretched this conversation to a point beyond normal return, but right here is the basis of my real issue. Instead of saying thank you, or when the doctor persisted with her friendliness, just smiling and moving on to eye chart two, I kept talking.

In all good social consciousness, it just wouldn't have been right to ignore the doctor. Ignoring my gastroenterologist, my manicurist, my pathologist, or my psychologist even would have been okay. But not my optometrist.

You see, I wasn't there for my stomach, or nails, or speech. And despite what others think, I wasn't out of my mind. I was there to get my focus in order.

Sue-Ellen, if I didn't say or do anything else, I had to tell the doctor I didn't have sneaks. Had not I spoken up, how else would the good doctor have ever known ...hell, I liked my damn pink suede shoes!

Gooood Morning

Speaking of being one burly orderly, a tailspin and a snap away from being committed, look at who's talking... gooood Morning.

Now before things get way out of hand, it needs to be pointed out; gooood Morning has done more for Early than anyone in the family. In fact, gooood Morning has done more for her family than any one else in the family, individually or collectively. That's what the good stands for.

gooood Morning is a good girl who cares a whole lot about her family. She cares so much about her family that sometimes her love feels suffocating.

No, really.

gooood Morning's showing of love actually has a real plastic bag and twisty tie feel to it. The family sometimes treaded like they were walking on thin ice around her. They had to tiptoe around her like this because although she would be the first at their bedside, she also might be the very one to have put them there.

But good grief, don't go to pulling the sweet child apart just yet. It really didn't take a magnifying glass to see her good heart. Okay, so you might have to stare real hard at her, but it wouldn't take an over active imagination to know she really did have a good heart.

Early knew best because Early lived with her. Early remembered how gooood Morning put up with her. And Early also remembered how passionate she was about defending the truth and protecting her integrity, even if it was at the risk of great peril to her. That's what put her so on edge, even if her goodness always stuck.

...like the day she and the Black Man went to blows.

Early couldn't believe it. Actually nobody could believe it. Whenever did a child get to see another birthday raising their hands to their father? Then again, we aren't talking about just any child. We are talking about gooood Morning with the cutting edge.

Don't touch her darn shoes. Don't stir that ugly bald-headed doll Shaddy. Hold back the wind. Don't let it get all up in her hair. And talking about Early... and Sue-Ellen... hello... will somebody please find the duct tape and tape that child's mouth shut, too.

No one could put a finger on what the argument gooood Morning and Early were having was about, but everyone remembers for sure the Black Man stepping in and the subsequent exchange.

He could care less which one of them had left the fingerprint on the table, or used the last drop of Windex, or left the mop in the dirty bucket of water. He just wanted them to shut up. And he wasn't waiting on Good Friday, or good and ready, or just whenever gooood Morning was good and tired of talking to shut up. The Black Man wanted the bickering to end, at the end of his last word.

gooood Morning however, wasn't through with her main point. Her points were always so vital and so very important to her. Or maybe it was the other way around. Maybe she was so vital and so very important to her points. Either way, they clung to each other like two drunks finagling ice on rollerblades.

The point was, Early had stepped on her good toes, and she wanted to be sure the Black Man had every cliff note he needed to get her point.

By this time, Early stopped talking. The Black Man just wasn't the ideal contender to go up against. Early had never seen an argument where he lost. Actually, for the sake of hanging on to an excellent point, Early didn't want to see a fight where the Black Man looked like he might lose.

gooood Morning could care less though. She held onto her drunken buddy and went word for word, telling the Black Man a thing or two. No amount of telling her to shut up was going to get her to shut up. She wasn't going to shut up even with the Black Man yelling at her, "Shut up!"

Instinctively Early stepped even further back. Early was like, "…whoa, it's about to get Baghdad whip-ass crazy up in here."

The sentiment cloaked the room. Carole, Sunday, Early, and all the flies clipped onto the screen door saw what was coming next. They didn't know how gooood Morning hadn't seen it too.

You couldn't hear a pin drop, but if gooood Morning had shut up you would have. She was just a huffing and puffing some kind of unbelievable. A few more sobering moments went by, the Black Man silent as a lamb. He stood there a lot longer than anyone imagined he ever would. And then there it came... the right hook.

Though no one wanted to believe the Black Man had actually reared back and hit gooood Morning in the chest if that wasn't what happened, but there was a slight whiff of air that passed by Early real quick like. It wasn't that two hit thing—the two hits where he hit her and she hit the floor. No, that's not what happened at all.

No joke and all be a monkey's right uncle, gooood

Morning was standing there upright and still very much uptight, let's get that straight. She was braced liked Cassius Clay, let's get that point straight as well. Her fists were bawled up, and close your eyes tight, because the girl was on her way to striking a note too.

The Black Man couldn't do nothing but laugh. He just looked at gooood Morning, shook his head, laughed, and walked away.

Sunday

Once upon a time Sunday was an altar boy. No one would put twenty dollars on that one. Sunday himself wouldn't have left any money on that one. He could be standing right at the altar wearing the acolyte robe and holding the church flag and he would pass on that bet.

A better bet for him would be the face maskless wearing halfback. Or, maybe something like a toothless, no kneepad flimsy shoulder pad sacked-back. Or, how about a Teeny Tiny walked over back. But, an altar Boy?

Nah, Sunday wouldn't bet on anything like that. But what's so bad about being an altar boy? After the way he got all knotted up about his church shoes when a hotheaded friend of his kicked them over, you'd think he'd have his chest poked all the way out being remembered as an altar boy. Like really, was squealing "hey man don't kick my church shoes" even necessary? Everybody knows 'hey man' and 'church shoes' don't hardly belong in the same sentence.

Whether Sunday admits it or not, once upon a time he really was an altar boy. The Black Man's family knew best. They saw him in that little red robe with the little white smock singing loud and proud 'This Little Light of Mine.' He was standing right in front of them... all lit up.

With his mouth opened wide and his eyes a glistening white, his little mighty light was just a shinning up the altar. The entire cold church got to see his big bright eyes, and his rows and rows of big pearly white teeth. Whether anyone knew it or not, but Sunday was gettin' in. The little fella was singing his way in.

That's probably what got the Reverend all worked up. "Ya' know Sunday, we sure could use a fella like you" is what the Reverend got to thinking. The reason the Black Man's family knew it was what the Reverend must have been thinking was because that's exactly what the Reverend said.

The Reverend wanted to use Sunday for a special project, which it took a whole lot of singing and lighting to be called upon by the highest noble authority of the church.

First the Reverend had to see the ray of hope. And then the Reverend had to walk up behind that ray of hope, and when least expected, ask that ray of hope how he would like to be granted the exclusive honor of lighting all the church candles for a special ceremony. When this happened, you were supposed to drop to your knees and respond.

"Oh yes, worshipful master, oh yes. Thank you for seeing me."

Now, you know Sunday don't want nobody knowing how he really responded. But all bets are on that it's a pretty safe bet he responded accordingly. It's a pretty safe bet because when the Black Man's family and the congregation took to their seats the following Sunday morning, hundreds of candles was wondrously lit.

Sunday hadn't missed a one. He lit all those candles without one utterance of repentance. But then of course too, everyone knows what happens when a person has to repent. They disappointed the anointed. You don't get to wear a red robe, with the white smock too, singing on the choir and being called an acolyte after being baptized and all, and not be about the business of unremitting, unrelenting service.

Good Lord, if your heart doesn't have you feeling some sense of obligation, then the Reverend's expression when you turned down his conferment sure as a weeping Jove should.

After the candles were lit, breathed over, and put out, the Reverend caught Sunday by a shoelace and started complimenting him again.

"Oh Sunday, it sure was a pleasure having you light those candles today. Oh Sunday, you did a marvelous job lighting each one of those candles. Oh Sunday, you handled yourself so well. Oh Sunday, you are growing into a fine tailored cloth. Oh Sunday, we are all so proud of you." On and on the Reverend complimented Sunday.

Sunday had to be about as happy as an altar boy could be. He was standing there just a beaming up the house of worship from the inside; the compliments just a swelling up his head for he hadn't been complimented like that never. That child was tearing everyone up he looked so happy. All that drinking wine, hanging out late and smoking weed and now he was officially gettin' in.

The ray of everlasting divinity turned to walk away. The boundless spray of sunshine had done his churchly duty; providing light forever... virtually sworn in now that he was all watted out. He could hang up the little red robe and... oh... what's that... the Reverend wasn't finished. The Reverend wanted to know how Sunday liked lighting all those candles.

Well, what was Sunday supposed to say?

"His arms got tired. Why was he pickin' on him? Lightin' all them candles sucked. Go to h—"

—Of course not. Sunday told the Reverend what any all watted out altar boy already sworn in was supposed to say. He said he liked lighting the candles just fine. But then after Sunday said what he was supposed to say and the Reverend said what he had in mind to say, why Sunday's bright light just died right out, right then and there.

The Reverend had Sunday lighting all them candles the following Sunday, and the Sunday following that Sunday, and every other third and fourth Sunday after that. And that was the last time the Black Man's family saw Sunday or his precious little church shoes ever again.

CHAPTER SIX

"Soft Pretzels & Cheesesteaks"

DER REITERS

She had seen the tremendous palace gardens in Bruhl, the spectacular cathedrals and castles peppering the Rhine, and even had the opportunity to stroll off the beaten path in cities as quaint and passive as Ettelbruck.

Her Big Sis and her Big Sis's friends zipped her up and down the autobahn giving her a chauffeured taste around the heart of Deutschland by private vehicle, by boat, by bus, and by Mercedes Funk Taxis, too.

She learned how well a Funk Taxi handled the curvaceous mountains, and acquainted herself with how friendly the cabby's could be too. They taught her nifty greetings such as, "guten Morgen," and "guten tag," and "tschus," or "auf Wiedersehen!"

She saw the rolling hills, the plains, and farms; chomped down on cutlets and fries dipped in mayonnaise at a few der schnellimbiss'; hung out at some of the local fests; and snacked on all the krapfens, strudels, der sauerbraten, bratwursts and sprudels she could hold down. She even had a beer or two at, at least one hoppenhouse.

In two weeks, with a stein, an anniversary clock, t-shirts, and several pieces of Eastern porcelain tucked in her souvenir bag she had seen, purchased, and done quite a bit for an eighteen year old who had never been out of America. She even had the chance to spend time with her niece and nephew who she hadn't seen in a couple of years. And yes, too, she also got to see how tempting it was to want to step on her niece's fat round feet for being so bad.

Auntie had a full vacation. It was time to trade in her leftover Deutsche Marks for American Dollars. It was time for Big Sis to get Auntie home.

But the airport was over four hours away from where Big Sis lived. Regardless of how fast those Funk Taxis drove, or how well the chauffeurs handled a Mercedes, it would have taken a whole lot of skill to shave off the amount of money Big Sis would need shaved off to afford a four hour chauffeured ride to Frankfurt. And yes, Big Sis might have been able to borrow a car, except the last thing Big Sis had driven was Rosemary. Scrounging up train fare to get Auntie to the airport was the only way to add a nice touch to winding down a bouquet European summer vacation.

Big Sis and Auntie awoke early, dropped the kids off with a sitter, and went by taxi to the train station. Big Sis used to live by the train station. She had purchased tickets from there going other places before. It therefore could be said Big Sis was somewhat familiar with how to get around Germany by train. Let's just say she knew a little more than the first week when she arrived. At least she wasn't going to end up covering Auntie on the ground because she thought the country was under attack.

This time around she would know the difference between American F16's on a routine maneuver, and the country being under attack. There would be no cringing embarrassment looking up at a busload of German passengers gaping out of windows, pointing and laughing at her huddled on the ground covering her children, waiting for bombs to go off in peacetime.

Big Sis purchased two tickets and waited with Auntie at the train station. It was a gorgeous day, so they sat outdoors between a sprawling farm and a bank of antiquated dwellings sitting tier-style before a thicket of woods. Beautiful. Each time they looked up at the sky they would be reminded that regardless of the distance soon to be between them, they would always be looking at the same sky.

After hoisting two full-grown pieces of luggage weighing fifty-pounds each aboard the train and taking their seats, Big Sis learned Auntie wasn't feeling well. Auntie got terrible cramps around that time of the month, which seemed to have picked up its ache at the very moment they boarded the train.

There had to be a better way of timing those womanly issues. A calendar, an alarm clock, a singing man, or telegram… anything that would bring out the Midol and make light of every woman's second most pressing issue all over the world. But it was too late for wishful thinking. They were already in route. Auntie was just going to have scoot over and allow Big Sis to share some of her pain.

Big Sis hoisted Auntie's suitcases in one of the overhead racks and then found that handsome chunk of a conductor who had taken the tickets.

Man, what an eye-full of a conductor he was. Six feet tall, deep engaging voice, strong jawbones, dark eyes, penetrating stare, all the way gorgeous this conductor was. And though the gracious chunk spoke fluent German, and no, Big

Sis did not speak an inch of German, but effortlessly she understood the chunk of a conductor to say, "S-t-a-y o-n t-h-e t-r-a-i-n u-n-t-i-l I t-e-l-l y-o-u t-o g-e-t o-f-f. I w-i-l-l l-e-t y-o-u k-n-o-w w-h-e-n t-o g-e-t o-f-f!" …Bleiben Sie auf dem Zug. And then…something like Ich werde abzusteigen was what he sort of yelled.

But he yelled it delectably though. Germans often talked like that—like they were angry or excited about something.

For the moment, Big Sis took in a little sigh. The conductor had comforted her; made her feel that she had nothing to worry about. Plus, Big Sis may have forgotten to mention, he looked good. He looked really, really, good. She wasn't sure if she had it right, but she was sort of thinking, Ich mag ihn. Wunderbar geldstrafestück!

Just like that Big Sis missed Auntie falling off into a deep sleep. But there. Big Sis had taken away some of Auntie's pain. Before long, between the quiet hum of the train trekking by unsullied pastures, and nice long lofty thoughts of the Wunderbar coupled with Auntie's undisturbed slumber, Big Sis got to feeling as if the train had purged its way over the legendary Wall and around two of Czech's border.

After a while, every stop where she could see more than two brick structures she started looking around; wondering if it was their stop. "Umm," she was thinking. "He might be cute, but he also might be forgetful." She had better lift her *arse* up to see for herself.

That was when a town so populated with stone structures it had to be Kaiserslautern popped into her viewfinder. Gently Big Sis shook Auntie and told her she thought it was their stop. She wasn't sure exactly when or where, but they were supposed to switch trains mid-route. This town looked like it might be the where.

Auntie peered out the window too, hanging over Big Sis's shoulder twice as wide-eyed. Save for the stick figures, hand signals, and creatures and characters on signs that expressed verboten—forbidden, anhalten—stop, and nein nicht gefahr—no, no, and hell no unless you want to be shot, they couldn't read a thing. Two wide-eyes turned into a hundred or more eyewitnesses.

Sure enough, there was the hunk on the platform. In long navy tails and high German boots, the conductor stood on the platform smoking a cigar with another conductor who looked like his twin. Big Sis didn't wait to finish surmising and assuming. She immediately grabbed both of Auntie's fifty-pound bags and told her to get moving.

Big Sis heard all about how trains in Germany didn't fool around. Like the poleizi and drivers on the autobahn, or drivers coming up on pedestrians caught in crosswalks, if there was one thing Big Sis learned quickly, and that was how to familiarize herself with the laws of Deutschland. That was one place where justice had no sympathy for ignorance of the law. The short end of one major law Big Sis knew well, and that was once the train's horn sounded, it wasn't stopping for nothing—last minutes passengers, almost missed stops, limbs, fingers, nothing!

The horn sounded just as Big Sis had both bags securely on the platform. She looked around like what a relief; and so what now? It was just about then when she caught sight of the conductor again, which had to be about the same time he caught sight of them.

As soon as their eyes met, the conductor started yelling. That time the cutie pie was really yelling. And the cutie pie was yelling in fluent German, too. Big Sis knew right away the cutie pie wasn't yelling and flailing his arms about to say, "hello you fine black American beauties come over here and chat and smoke it up with us."

The conductor was yelling nein nicht gefahr words. And Big Sis knew just what those words meant. She didn't have to speak the language to know he was saying, "Get your auf black asses back on the train," followed by "…and don't get off until I say so." The necessary exclamations followed each of the phrases.

See, it was that easy to understand the language. No translator needed. Auntie understood this too. In two healthy, feeling much better strides, Auntie was back on the train. Meanwhile, on the platform was Big Sis tussling and haggling with two stubborn pieces of luggage.

Big Sis was down there on the platform with the train engines grunting and grumbling, and her thinking… okay, so forget what Big Sis was thinking… but she was down there huffing and puffing, looking like a hundred-pounds was dragging her instead of the other way around. Desperately her eyes pleaded with Auntie's eyes looking pathetically down on her in doorway.

Big Sis was so sure Auntie could read, "please help me," furrowed between the deep creases in her forehead. After all, they both spoke perfect Black English.

"Get die säcke bitch!" was what desperately skidded out of Big Sis's mouth.

Why in a silly blank stare was Auntie standing there looking down at her anyway? And hey, you 8th and 9th wonders of a Roman Empire, nothing was hardly that funny. Big Sis was in real trouble standing there on the platform amid long horns, whistles blowing, engines revving, and two large suitcases blocking her feet. Big Sis was down there on the platform consumed with thoughts of what being left in Mississippi 1963 inside Auschwitz actually looked like.

Huffing and puffing, hurling one bag after the other on the train, and diving onboard herself, Big Sis went on and did the good sport thing. She stood, brushed her knees, and again took another bow of embarrassment.

Mr. Romance

One evening while sitting in the middle of a potato patch doing what he liked doing most, earning his keep while thumbing through a newspaper, Mr. Romance came across a pretty good size ad advertising Richard Pryor and Eddie Murphy—side by side—starring in an upcoming movie.

Mr. Romance didn't get excited about much, but Eddie and Richard flanked side by side made him pulled up his socks and straighten his cap. He didn't even wait for the punch line. Right then and there he started laughing. Sitting in the middle of a potato patch on the lookout for potato robbers he knew a quite a bit about good comedy.

In an unprecedented move he called his conceited stuck-up girlfriend—that would be Supercilious—right away. He was still laughing when she picked up the telephone. In a hearty chuckle he let her know he was taking her to see Eddie and Richard really cut up.

"Oh?" Supercilious was surprised. Mr. Romance

wasn't one to call out-of-the-blue offering to splurge on something like a middle of the workweek movie date. That wasn't his style. Like the other dates—to a park that sat in the center of town overlooking a brook, and to the other park that sat just on the other side of that park—Mr. Romance was more of a simple man.

Come Wednesday evening he had washed, and oiled, and gassed up Nellie. Now that was more like his style. He was a one-two-three type of man who liked everything in order. Every time he took her on a date, Nellie had to be right. That was step two in his lane of order. The third step was him showing up his usual overly early self.

He walked in the door to find Supercilious, like her normal self, not ready. True he had given her a whole two days to have lined up her eyeliner and select a color; and to pick out her favorite nail polish and play musical chairs with her shoes, but she still wasn't ready. Two days still wasn't enough time.

He should have known that. Heck, the first time they had gone out, he showed up five or ten minutes early. Of course then, she was running around the house hurling hair rollers in one direction, her bathrobe in another direction, and insults in the other.

The next date he showed up thirty-minutes before he said he would pick her up. Well hell, that time she was still standing in line at the supermarket. And the next thing she knew, he was showing up at least an hour or more before dates. Most of the time then, she wasn't even out of bed.

Now here he was at the back door tapping his foot a whopping two hours early! Was he out of his friggin' mind? The movie started in, 'oh... another few hours', which he managed to squish down inside an hour worrying about things like traffic and parking.

Call it logic or sarcasm, but on a Wednesday night in a town populated by a scant thousand people or so, which included the sick and shut in, and a three-lane highway... come on now... traffic? In five years there had yet to be one traffic jam so debilitating that had her scarred remembering it.

She rushed out the door with Mr. Romance all swelled up about the possibility of getting stuck in gridlock traffic, and then not getting good seats. It didn't make for the nicest ride, but at least Mr. Romance was a gentleman opening and closing doors for her. It was the least she could be thankful for since she had her make-up bag, purse, and shoes in one hand, and bra in the other.

She put the bra on first, and then the shoes. But when she got to applying the make-up, she had to deal with Mr. Romance twitching up his face because he didn't like her using the passenger visor mirror to see with. In his lane of order the visor had to sit in a certain position at all times. Just seeing it move in another direction disrupted his train of thought.

She went on and used the mirror anyway, until she caught him gawking out the window, oogling another woman who he obviously thought looked better. Oooo! It was dark out and the windows were tinted, but she slapped the visor down and turned it sideways to see if it would help him regain his train of thought.

They got to the theatre with that chunk of an hour left to kill. This was even after Mr. Romance had driven Nellie all five miles at a funeral's pace, and circled the town not once or twice, but three times looking for the parking lot.

She laughed to herself. Some men were funny, and then some were hilarious. Mr. Romance was a riot. They walked up to the ticket counter where a woman in the ticket booth had to open the venation blinds to inform Mr. Romance that tickets for the next show would go on sale thirty minutes prior to the current show ending. This meant they would have to wait, oh... oh, another whole hour.

See!?! He was a riot. He couldn't get this information from her—like before they left the house. He had to hear it from a ticket lady—after the rushing, and the oogling, and the near break-up just getting there.

So now whadda' ya' know he decides to do with this whole whopping hour they had left to kill? He decides to kill the hour by heading over to a supermarket to buy snacks. The theatre snacks were too costly he concluded. She nodded in agreement. Wasn't much to say there. Theatre snacks were pricey. It ranked at the top ten of chief theatre complaints.

He selected a few snacks, and even turned around to consult with her. "Oh, by the way... did you want something?" Quietly Supercilious shook her head no and marched right behind him back to Nellie. They arrived at the theatre with just enough spare time to spend thirty minutes easily, waiting in Nellie for the show to let out.

Back in the parking lot they are only two people in a car talking about movie theatre policies on permitting food and drinks inside theatres. A riot avalanching downhill.

Supercilious brought up the subject. She didn't know of a theatre in America that allowed picnic spreads in Pic-n-Save bags inside theatres. Mr. Romance however, thought it was no one's business where he bought his refreshments. But if theatres really cared, they should do a little price comparison-shopping around the neighborhood. They might learn a thing or two; such as how ridiculously high priced their snacks were. Supercilious laughed—out loud.

That did it. She had managed to ruin the date. Mr. Romance jumped out of Nellie and slammed the door, which tickled her even more.

Back at the ticket window it was finally time to purchase the tickets. And yes, Mr. Romance was still paying. That's what men do when they are out on a date and behaving.

He pulled out his fat, rather odd-looking cumbersome wallet and fumbled with it as if it was gold. The odd-looking wallet wouldn't open correctly. The ends kept curling up around a stack of evidence tracing his entire life. She could tell some of the stuff stuffed in his wallet had been there long before him. She definitely knew the picture of his grandpa was there before him.

She stepped back and allowed him the elbowroom he needed to dig and dig.

There was no visor so it must have been the gawking that caused him to loose his train of thought. As soon as he had gotten oh... maybe elbow deep into his wallet looking for his oldest five-dollar bill, was it when he suddenly remembered the coupon.

Coupon?

Good Lord, Mr. Romance had a coupon—a coupon that was to knock off a few dollars off the movie's grand total. One of them was getting in free.

Supercilious started looking around. Why hadn't she thought about wearing a shawl or a cape or something. Using her hands to cover her face would have been just a little too obvious. She stepped even further back to allow him more room. It looked like he was going to need a little more room than elbowroom. How about shoulder room and room enough for a left hook and a backhand swing.

He couldn't find the newspaper clipping. His wide wallet was opened up to his neck and it still wasn't there. That's how she and the ticket lady got to see his granddaddy's picture, and all the other evidence outlining his life.

Okay, so if the coupon wasn't in his wallet, then it must have been in one of his pockets. But which one? He moved on to his pockets… the deep pockets holding the snacks he purchased. He scrounged around the bottom of his pockets long enough to realize time was just a ticking.

"Hurry! Hurry!" That was Supercilious tapping her foot. "Remember that mob you thought was going to beat you to the parking lot, well they are now all lined up behind you."

Eventually he gave up. There was no shame in his game. She may have been embarrassed, with her stuck-up conceited self, but he wasn't. He had every right to save every dime he could. It was his money to do with as he pleased.

That's a Roger. Mr. Romance pulled out that honey bun, a bag of chips, a snicker bar, and a can of soda. As deep as he was digging, he could have also pulled out a few bananas, four oranges, and one conveyor belt of red apples and yellow onions too. She couldn't recall everything, but she recalled how large the ticket lady's eyes grew watching with open-mouthed awe each non-perishable he brought out for inspection.

The ticket lady shrieked, "Ugh Sir, you can't bring that in here!"

Piggy Packin' Bears

Mama Bear looked here, and Mama Bear looked there. She looked high, and she looked low. Mama Bear looked everywhere for her good set of jewels before telling Papa Bear and her baby cubs it was time to pack it up and go. If she couldn't find her jewels in the place where she expected them to be, then she didn't want to be there no more. She'd rather just get up and go.

Though Mama Bear put everyone on notice, it was Papa Bear who had done the plotting and planning. That's how Papa Bear was. He had been to a few paratrooper schools in his career—Hard Knocks I, II, and III. No one could tell Papa Bear a thing. Graphing out a move like this was right up his alley. He couldn't wait to put those skills to use.

For too long he'd been looking for the moment to jump back into uniform. During an electrical storm he tried, but then the storm only lasted a few hours. He tried using his skills during an Earthquake too, but then they were already hunkered down, and the government was dishing out free supplies too. At every wakening turn Papa Bear had never been fully able to deploy his skills. Not until Mama Bear announced she was fed up and ready to move on.

Now he wasn't expecting to be jumping from airplanes or anything like that. He was just aiming to teach his new recruits how to hunker down, follow rules, and how to live on edge and survive.

So while Mama Bear got to prettying up the packing boxes labeling and taping the seams just right, Papa Bear outfitted his map with lots of red circles, marking the locations where they would eat, lodge, and even take all of their potty breaks. Papa Bear couldn't wait. Tapping his foot and making his head dance, he was finally going to put his paratrooper skills to some fine useful use. He had things all worked out...

...well, all except three little things.

DAY 1. ONE *HELLUVA* RIDE

Not that it needs pointing out, but right from the start Mama Bear and her cubs let it be known they hadn't been to paratrooper school. Mama Bear and her cubs hadn't even been to hard luck school. The only school they had been to was the school of futuristic opportunities and advancement.

This was the school where they were taught to reach for the stars, but aim for the moon, not like in Papa Bear's school where he was just taught to aim high. To Mama Bear that aiming high sounded a whole lot like reaching for a shelf just above her head. Mama Bear was looking to go further than that. That's how Mama Bear got to thinking about getting up and going in the first place. Futuristic school put this type of thinking in her head.

Right from the start Mama Bear pulled out of the driveway well off course. No sooner than she had closed the car door good, was it when she started flipping through one of her favorite lessons—exploring all the what ifs. That's how Mama Bear was. She was always exploring the what ifs. Never mind Papa Bear's explicit instructions: "Go to the bank and then meet me at the Stop-n-Go just after the underpass off Highway 1."

Those were the only instructions Papa Bear had given Mama Bear. He hadn't said any more, and no less. He certainly said nothing about rushing to the bank, and then waiting for him at the top of a hill to see how the truck was fairing with pulling the trailer. Nothing of the sort came out of his mouth.

The truck and the trailer were performing just fine. Papa Bear already had done all the checks. Any abundantly necessary maintenance work had already been performed. So that really was none of Mama Bear's concern.

What should have been of utmost importance to Mama Bear however; what she needed to be paying attention to was Papa Bear's simple straightforward instructions. He needed her to meet him at the Stop-n-Go, as instructed. Nothing more and nothing less.

But Mama Bear wasn't thinking about no Stop-n-Go or underpass off Highway 1. As usual, Mama Bear had gotten busy with all of that what if thinking.

What if Mama Bear drove real fast to the bank and then real fast to the top of the hill, and then sat there and waited for Papa Bear to come over the hill? From where she had pulled off the road, she'd have a real clear view of how the trailer was performing.

What if the trailer didn't look like it had what it would take to make it the rest of the 2999-mile journey? Then what? They'd have to turn around and shoot for another day.

What Mama Bear didn't know however, Papa Bear had long ago cleared the top of the hill... long before Mama Bear had even put her ATM card into the ATM machine slot.

Mama Bear got worried. She was so worried about Papa Bear not coming over that hill that she got to thinking even more. What if Papa Bear had run off and left her? That's what Mama Bear was saying aloud. "What if Papa Bear had said forget this trip and forget me!" ...In fact, what if Papa Bear wished he'd never met her, or those cubs. He probably hated her cubs. He probably hadn't planned on meeting them anywhere. In fact, "what if he hoped to never see us again?"

See. Even Mama Bear's cubs thought her thinking was

funny. She just thought entirely too much. Papa Bear hadn't been thinking no such thing. Papa Bear waited nearly thirty minutes for Mama Bear and her cubs to show up at the Stop-n-Go. He was waiting right at the designated meeting point, where he had specifically asked her to be.

Mama Bear disobeying Papa Bear like that threw the first noose in his plan. Before they had gotten good and started, Mama Bear had already put them behind schedule by nearly thirty minutes or more.

But Mama Bear wasn't done with the thinking. She got to thinking more and more. If Papa Bear wasn't going to leave them, then perhaps he was going to try killing them. He certainly had the training.

For miles, all that lay ahead of them were zigzagged one-lane highways so dusty she thought for sure she was driving on sand. Papa Bear had taken them a back route—a ferocious hot punishing back route—so punishing Mama Bear was calling it the Mojave Desert.

And to really apply pressure, Papa Bear requested that Mama Bear refrain from using the air conditioner. In Papa Bear's paratrooper militarism dictionary that meant: Do Not Use. Papa Bear was going to make decorated soldiers out of them yet.

Mama Bear tried to comply, but it wasn't easy wrestling with Mojave heat in the middle of the day. It was so hot Mama Bear could swear the sun was even melting. Mama Bear couldn't see a thing. Nothing but a torrential rain of dust and heat sprayed before her. That's how a coal carrying train nearly liked to have grinded them into fine baking powder.

All that saved them from being rolled over by forty or more iron wheels of steel was the train's bells and whistles screaming to a bloody carnage, and a good set of brakes. So yes, Mama Bear needed to suck up some of that AC. That was just going to have to be Papa Bear's toll for taking them through Mojave Canyon's death-gripping back door.

At the first stop, a gas station so small Mama Bear had no idea how Papa Bear managed to draw a circle around it on a map, she berated Papa Bear for taking them the treacherous route. Could he not read a map?

The thin blue lines stood for something. It meant treacherous. Not for family excursions. Avoid at all cost. Papa Bear should have learned all this in that fine paratrooper school he bragged about belonging to. How to stay alive had to be the main lesson taught. Mama Bear fussed about the treacherous route until Papa Bear slid from beneath Mama Bear's car. He wanted to know if she had been running Nellie poo's air conditioner.

Mama Bear hesitated. The question stumped her. Mama Bear, of course, remembered when she needed the AC, but now that she could breathe and was able to give Papa Bear a piece of her mind, she had forgotten about Papa Bear's instructions not to run the AC.

Mama Bear was going to have to get creative. Mama Bear was going to have to lie. So she, too, peeked beneath Nellie poo. She didn't know what she was looking for, but she at least wanted to seem concerned. No she hadn't used the AC. Hadn't he seen her all two hundred miles with her head hanging out of the window panting for air?

Day 2. Playing *the* Mind Games

At sunup Papa Bear reminded Mama Bear and the cubs they had 2697 miles to go and were one state off schedule. That was Mama Bear's doing.

Mama Bear had emphatically promised Papa Bear she could drive 600 miles a day. That had been the lynch pin in most of his plotting and planning.

But then three hundred and some odd miles down the road, and they were checking into a hotel. But that was Papa Bear's fault though. He shouldn't have taken them through the Mojave Desert. Had Mama Bear known Papa Bear was going to take them through a canyon like Mojave, she would have told him she could possibly do thirty miles a day. That way he would have found another route. How about that?

So here they were, at sunup, checking out of a hotel where one of its own postcards read: Between 300 miles from hell and 3000 miles to nowhere. Mama Bear liked that postcard. She went right for her purse and bought it while Papa Bear was outside stretching and flexing.

Papa Bear loved catching that early morning sun like that. That's when the air was the stillest and the quietest; when right after completing several rounds of his preferred calisthenics—back bends, arm curls, and neck rolls—he jogged over more of his plotting and planning.

Mama Bear saw him out there. But while he was doing his calisthenics, she got to doing her thinking. Good Lord, what did that man have in store for them that day? Mama Bear never could tell with Papa Bear. One week when an earthquake had blacked out the city, taking out all the gas pumps and grocery stores in the area, Papa Bear had them eating sea rations.

Papa Bear had pitched a tent right in the middle of the living room and had the house all lit up with chemical lights, piling brown vacuumed-packed food pouches like sand bags all around the tent. All her and the cubs needed was a helmet and a pair of boots… and a rifle perhaps.

That's how Papa Bear was. He knew how to cook hot meals without electricity, and he knew how to make a quarter tank of gas last a week. When times were the toughest, Papa Bear always had an extra trick up his sleeve.

The only problem was, when there were no problems, Papa Bear would invent problems, just to test his skills. That's what troubled Mama Bear most. Just what kind of trouble was he going to invent next.

Papa Bear hopped into the truck pulling the trailer, and Mama Bear hopped into Nellie poo totting the cubs. Mama Bear promised herself she wouldn't stir Papa Bear into making trouble. She was going to be on her best behavior. She even was going to try surprising Papa Bear by doing 600 miles, hopefully more.

And then a few good miles down the road, Mama Bear started thinking again. She was thinking just how sleepy she was. She wanted to jump in the back seat with the cubs she was so sleepy. Maybe Papa Bear had stashed toothpicks somewhere in the car. Papa Bear did things like that too. He always stashed necessities no one would think about. Mama Bear could bet that if she called Papa Bear right at that moment, he would be able to tell her just where to find toothpicks in the car.

But Mama Bear didn't call Papa Bear. Toothpicks weren't going to help her. And she for dang sure wasn't going to let Papa Bear know that she needed to pull over and close her eyes for a few hours. Already they had 2693 miles to go, and were still that one state off schedule. Whatever way Mama Bear got word to Papa Bear, she was going to have to make it interesting. Oh, she knew what she could do.

Mama Bear sighed and allowed the car to drift across the double yellow lines, and then slowly sift back behind Papa Bear. Not sure if he had seen her, she did it again. She drifted and then sifted, only that time she drifted and sifted a few seconds longer than before. When she thought she caught Papa Bear looking, she drifted and sifted a third time, dramatically, just to be sure.

Now, one thing to note about Papa Bear, his radar could read into a tactical procedure like a covert ambush into Normandy. He would understand the significance of the sifting and drifting. Yep, she saw the flicker... no secret there. His blinker was going, signaling he was allowing an unscheduled rest stop to break the stride in his strategy.

Mama Bear obediently followed Papa Bear. They pulled into a hotel parking lot where Papa Bear slowly got out of the truck and walked towards her. Mama Bear laughed to herself. Even with all the reading into tactical procedures there was no way he was going to see this one coming. Paratrooper school didn't teach stuff like this.

Mama Bear rolled down the window and sleepily as she was, looked Papa Bear 'round about the eyes and said, "You must be tired too, huh?"

Day 3. Look *Out!* Traylla!

By day three Mama Bear and her cubs were having a ball—a miscellaneous still one state off, three hundred more miles shaved off kind of a ball. Day 3 turned into a pit stop fun kind of day.

First it was Mama Bear with the great caffeine intake trying to stay awake. All that driving helped Mama Bear learn something new about herself. She was no good before noon. There also was a little bit of an issue with the cubs' pint size bladders, too. One six-ounce cup of anything liquid equaled roughly fifteen potty breaks. That's how traylla joined the fun.

The first couple of times Mama Bear pulled over, Papa Bear hadn't needed as much notice. With daylight hanging over the highway and the highway practically deserted, abruptly stopping hadn't been too much trouble. Papa Bear had been able to leisurely hang his head out of the window, and in his formal Southern drawl, drag out 'traaaylla'.

It tickled the cubs silly laughing at Papa Bear communicating whole big concepts using just one word. And then night fell, and convoys of 18-wheelers began taking over the road like a slumber sleepover trucker's convention. Papa Bear was taking the pit stopping a whole lot more seriously then. The smell of jake brakes sucking up whopping chunks of air passing over the highway meant something to him.

The sulfured smelling air meant nothing to Mama Bear however. That was a concern for whosever tires were on fire and didn't know it. Mama Bear and the cubs weren't paying the jakers and brakers no mind. They got to giggling once more about the need to make another pit stop.

"Here we go again…" Mama Bear used her manners and pulled alongside Papa Bear, with an 18-wheeler closing in on her, explicitly motioning that she needed to pull over. Papa Bear looked at Mama Bear, nodded, and then maneuvered into the lead position.

"Wow, that was easy," Mama Bear sighed. Papa Bear was lightening up. Sometimes Papa Bear wasn't so bad. Sometimes he held back the militarism. Sometimes he was almost human. This looked like one of his humane moments.

And then all be damned if Papa Bear didn't pass the next exit. Papa Bear whizzed by the exit as if the exit didn't exist. But wait… "What if Papa Bear hadn't understood her urgency?" Papa Bear probably thought it wasn't a good exit.

The next exit was a good exit. The bright emblem of golden arches told Mama Bear it was a great exit. Mama Bear stayed behind Papa Bear and hit her turning blinkers.

And what do know? Papa Bear passed that exit too—knowing good and cherry well blasted he had seen Mama Bear's blinker panting for dear life.

Mama Bear was getting desperate. The cub in the back

seat was having a hissy fit about needing to *use it*. Mama Bear had to tell the cub seated beside her to write Papa Bear a note: We Need Gas Now.

The cub grabbed a pencil and piece of paper and wrote away. Mama Bear moved into the left lane preparing to drive alongside Papa Bear so the cub could display the note in the window. But Mama Bear found the faster she drove, the faster Papa Bear drove.

"Would you look at this fool?" Papa Bear was driving like he had somewhere to be. He thought she was gonna pass him and make another traylla stop. Papa Bear's militarism often had him acting silly like that. All Mama Bear really was trying to do was get lined up with Papa Bear so the cub could put the note in the window.

Mama Bear, believe it or not, was trying to do the right thing. But Papa Bear wouldn't slow down. At least twice Mama Bear had to fall behind Papa Bear to allow a blaring, bearing down 18-wheeler to pass. On the third try Mama Bear wasn't bull jiving around. She really stepped on it.

She pulled alongside Papa Bear and had the cub hold the note up to the window. That time Papa Bear had his face all scrunched up and was acting like he couldn't read the note. Papa Bear wasn't falling for the note. He knew exactly how much gas was in this car. He wasn't going to stop, and that was all there was to it. Mama Bear wanted to remove one of her flip-flops and throw it in his direction, but another semi moved her out of the way.

Well, that was it. Mama Bear had tried. She had tried everything she knew of to get Papa Bear to stop. Mama Bear had no choice. After all, it's like they say, 'when they had to go, they had to go.'

Mama Bear knew what she had to do. Mama Bear whizzed right on by Papa Bear lugging that trailer and pulled over at the first clearing she spotted. Gravel and road debris kicked up from beneath Mama Bear's wheels and washed Papa Bear's windows, front and back. The cubs cried laughing. The trailer whizzed on by with Papa Bear hanging far out of the window yelling, "traaaaaaaayyyyylllla!"

Mama Bear got scolded good for that pit stop though. Papa Bear just couldn't allow Mama Bear to keep stopping like that. And no, Papa Bear hadn't seen any note. But no wonder. Mama Bear had to squint to read the note, too. And she was squinting using her 20/20 vision; without the blaring horns of 18-wheelers demanding she get out of the way. What had the cub used to write the note with? An eraser?

DAY 4. TOO *MUCH* TELEVISION

Day 4 found Papa Bear a much happier camper. It was a Kodak kind of day. Papa Bear could smell it. They had breezed on into familiar Lone Ranger territory. Papa Bear recognized the scent right away. Fertilizer. He loved that scent. For him it meant one, and only one thing. Home sweet home.

Now it was Papa Bear's turn to laugh.

First was first. They were having brunch at Bob Evan's all you can eat country boy diner. Second; dinner was going to be at the Cracker Barrel. And finally, they were hunkering in at an off-the-beaten-path bunker.

Papa Bear couldn't wait. He was rubbing his hands together and swaying side-to-side, flexing and stretching and doing all the teasing calisthenics he liked to do. This was going to be his day. Recognizable nourishment, reminiscing on the way things used to be, and scaring the all-aspiring hell out of Mama Bear and her darling little cubs was next on his agenda.

The cubs weren't laughing even a little bit. Their eyes were as big as twin saucers when they saw Papa Bear pulling into the Cracker Barrel. Why was Papa Bear doing this to her cubs? Papa Bear knew good and frankin' well the cubs would not want to eat where they could swear locals were rocking on porches expressing their God given right to bear arms.

Papa Bear knew the cubs were frightened. They heard the stories, seen the movies, and read the scripts. Whenever had a town whose name read like the first sentence in a terrifying Huckleberry novel ever been known to be hospitable to futuristic little cubs with great thinking capabilities?

Mama Bear tried not to stir Papa Bear by laughing, but she couldn't help it. Why had Papa Bear crossed over the railroad tracks? Papa had by-passed every two dollar chicken, taco, and rib shack on the East side of the tracks. He had gone out of his way, clearly off the beaten path, to eat at a place that added miles back onto the schedule.

Papa Bear didn't care nothing about making up for lost time. Papa Bear just liked stirring up trouble. He wanted to have a reason to be needed. Mama Bear tried keeping a straight face, but she just couldn't hold onto the giggle any longer. Is *"Just Get Us The Hell Out Of Here"* the next town over?

Papa Bear got hot. That was the absolute last straw. He was tired of fooling around with those damn cubs and Mama Bear, too. He needed to turn up the heat. When new recruits messed up, they got to peel extra potatoes, wash the ceiling, or break up cement. Mama Bear and her cubs were getting the real hunkering down at an off-the-beaten-path bunker detail. There. That's what Papa Bear was fixin' to do.

There would be plenty chickens in the coop to feed and then eat. All they had to do was catch the chickens and then wring their necks. They could laugh all they wanted while chasing down their meal. And they could stop, drop, and roll, making all the pit stops their little warrior bladders desired—wherever and whenever they pleased too. That'll fix 'em. That'll fix 'em good!

Day 5. Gettin' *to the* Jewels

Sure enough, the cubs beat daybreak getting up. Before Papa Bear had spread toothpaste all the way over his toothbrush the cubs were sitting in the car closed mouth and eyes glued to the window—waiting. They weren't messing around with Papa Bear no more. He had their attention. They were ready to find Mama Bear a good set of new jewels.

But Papa Bear didn't have Mama Bear's attention. By day five Mama Bear was as tired as a whole can of tunas festering in oyster sauce. Her thinking had slowed way down, nearly to a grinding halt. Mama Bear wasn't even thinking about those darn jewels by day five.

Instead, Mama Bear was looking down at that smeared 300/3000 mile postcard she brought along for the extra cheer. Ump. What a way to go. Let her find out all that time they had been driving backwards.

At a rest stop circled on the third page of Papa Bear's map, Mama Bear pulled up alongside Papa Bear with one eye half shut, and the other eye half open. She had barely put Nellie in park when she let one of the cubs out. Her foot was sort of idling between the gas pedal and brake pedal... like how five-speeds idled, except Nellie poo wasn't no five-speed.

Mama Bear was pooped and Papa Bear knew it. He had worn Mama Bear down and straightened out her little darling cubs. The rest of the journey was all his. He could pull out his plotted up atlas and get real cute with it. Mama Bear and her cubs weren't throwing him off schedule no more.

Papa Bear stood between the truck and Nellie poo flexing and stretching. It wasn't morning, but he also flexed and stretched like that after conquering a great feat.

Drumming up chummy pointless chitchat waiting for one of the cubs to return, Papa Bear completed a few more neck rolls and side curls while Mama Bear sat in Nellie poo with her head resting forward on the steering wheel.

Mama Bear was hardly paying Papa Bear much attention. She just wanted to get to wherever they were supposed to be getting to, which when she did, she hoped she would remember what kind of jewels she was looking for.

Suddenly Mama Bear hears "Excuse me" rattling from somewhere off to her left, interrupting absolutely nothing.

Mama Bear wanted to lift up to see what the rattling was and where it was coming from but her nerve endings were taking a long time to fire up.

The rattling came again. "Who's driving that trailer?"

Mama Bear took a little peek. Sure enough, standing to her left was a half-alive man dressed in a suffocating brown jumpsuit holding a broom in one hand, and maybe a rake in the other. Park Services was what the patch on the suffocating brown jumpsuit read; and Park Services was looking at her.

Mama bear still couldn't form a lot of words, but some of her thinking was coming back. Unless Park Services thought she was ambidextrous, or that she had zapped off a hi-fi sci-fi screen and wandered down to Earth, she couldn't possibly be driving the trailer sitting in Nellie poo... with her foot still idling between the brake pedal and the gas pedal. Nellie poo was in every bit of a position to keep on rolling right over the broom, the rake, the creased up finger and the park services patch too. Nellie poo could have done all this.

The next thing Mama Bear heard was, "She did."

Now hold up. That rattle was coming from her left too, but it wasn't Park Services. Why... that was Papa Bear's rattle tooting. When Mama Bear looked up again, Papa Bear was easing back. He had stopped with the side curls and neck rolls, and he wasn't grinning anymore either. Papa Bear saw it coming—Mama Bear was about to unzip her head from the back, so he got to moving that trailer.

...And still she gets to hear, "Ugh, you can't park that trailer there like that. These spaces are for cars. You have to park that trailer with the trucks... over there!"

The trailer was moving while Park Services quivering creased up finger was still pointing. See, these were the instances that revved up Mama Bear's thinking. Was Park Services kidding or that slow?

Maybe Park Services was angry about not being able to

get all the dirt from beneath his toenails when he woke up that morning. Or maybe his knees had stopped hurting, and now it was the macula in one of his optic nerves acting up. What if someone had given Park Services a whole lot of authority, but no instructions. Or just maybe, how about if Park Services had borrowed the suffocating brown jumpsuit, highjacked the rake and broom, and was using a fictitious name?

Mama Bear didn't play around with the answers to all her maybes and what ifs. She was too hot, too pooped, and not in a too good of a thinking mood.

"Well at least God loves me," Park Services retorted.

Mama Bear smiled. After clapping trains, a ferocious punishing hot sun, 18-wheelers, and half a town expressing their God given right to bear arms, did Park Services really think that she wasn't loved too? Shucks, there were jewels right there.

"...and God loves me too!"

CHAPTER SEVEN

"Little Quakers"

ANY FOOL

Now any fool should know Momma's son was as smart as a whip. And sure, like most mommas, Momma held this sentiment high above her son's head, too. All mommas did. All mommas thought their child was the smartest.

Their child won first place in the spelling B contest, the art contest, a poetry contest, and had their brilliant novel read by a literary giant. They had been hailed valedictorian of their kindergarten class, had played the piano—solo—for a grand symphony… and on and on down a list they could go. From the day the child arrived, that child was like a little goddess carved right from a shrines turret... just like Momma's son, except... Momma's son really was smarter.

Ask anyone. And heck, if you don't believe them, ask him. That young man had all the answers. He knew if A was B, then A couldn't be C, so then why try forcing C into A if A was B. Even when his answers didn't pan all the way out, he had a solution for that one too. Momma's son always had someone on hand to blame. Like he told his Momma, it was better that way. That way any fool would know he was always right.

Despite this insight Momma loved her son, and still thought he was beyond average bright. She told anyone who had ears all about how intelligent and sharp he was.

He was good in Math. His Reading scores were unmatched. A science teacher handpicked him to participate in a science camp. He made another year on the honor roll. His SAT scores had come in. Every worthy college in the country was looking at him. His IQ had been tested. Surprise! Her child was a genius.

He also used to play basketball. Now he played first string cornerback for his high-school football team. Momma couldn't have been prouder of her extremely talented and gifted son. It therefore should go without saying, Momma held out high hopes for that child. That son of hers one day was going to be someone. He was going to make her a really proud momma.

And then Momma's son turned eighteen. He was still very bright, even if he had turned the tables on Momma somewhat. Kids always do that though. Why, Momma had done the same thing to her momma.

Kids always got yae so grown and then started thinking their momma didn't know much. Momma found herself sometimes having to ask if she had even given birth to that boy, or if he had birthed her. Something was definitely very, very wrong for him to be walking around her house talking about hanging around for a year past graduation, and maybe working for a while.

Now Momma had taught him better than that. She really hadn't been bull jiving around when she told him long before he started turning his knowledge onto her, there would only be two sets of papers lying on the table. Scientific calculator, or no scientific calculator, she was doing the math for him.

Either he was joining the military, or he was going to college. And any fool would know how all that added up. Either or way, he was getting out of Momma's house.

Momma's son ignored her though. What did Momma know? He was the smart one. Not her. She was just bluffing. That's what mommas sometimes did when they didn't know as much as their children. They bluffed and bullied their kids into making decisions that would keep their egos afloat.

Momma could go on as she always did, huffing and bluffing, and blowing off steam. Like he said, he was hanging around the house after graduation to sort out his next steps. Maybe if he could, he might work, and then he might not. He wasn't old like her. That was her silly mistake. Now she had to work. He was a kid and still had time to make up his mind.

Like it or not and whatever the case, this was his tentative plan. He was just going to go on and do as he always did, outsmarting her. Just wait and see. She would see.

But Momma really was serious. Any fool should know Momma didn't play like that. Momma could care less what other people were saying; talking about how bad and sad the military was. The military wasn't any sadder than the havoc going on in neighborhoods flooded with shiftless, out-of-work, non-educated, and not to mention undisciplined young bums. That's exactly what Momma called them—her son included—young, trifling, out of work bums.

War might be bad, but war wasn't the only way the military used these young men. Soldiers were deployed for hurricanes, floods, earthquakes, bridges collapsing, asphalt laying, and yes, civil unrest too. The military kept hoodlums off the streets and busy with many useful assignments.

That child certainly wasn't going to be dragging around her house in his filthy underpants and crusty mouth talking about looking for a job—maybe—one day next week.

Momma's son however, was persistent. Smart children usually are. That child told Momma all about the military. The military was for mechanical cataleptic people who didn't mind opening their mouths to have orders poured down their throats. They were slow moving unmentionables with spit-shined anonymous objectives that marched to unknown destinations for unspecified reasons.

None of his friend's parents forced them to join the military. No parent in their right mind would. All of his friends were given cars—luxury cars—after graduation. And that was whether they graduated or not. None of his friends got the boot out the door.

...And?

Momma knew all this. But if that child who she had so courteously given birth to, and loved, and held high hopes for didn't get to minding her orders, then he was going to fit right in—with the unmentionables.

Whether he ended up polishing shoes in a brig, somewhere along Pennsylvania Avenue, or where all the soldiers polished their boots, he was going to be a shoe shining fool if he didn't take his tail to school. Now any fool should have known Momma was dead serious. Momma didn't play around when she talked like that. She meant every word.

And hey look, if things didn't pan all the way out, then Momma's son would get his wish—someone to blame.

Any fool should know the argument didn't end there. Bright early one workday morning when Momma was supposed to be at work, she took off from work. Momma hated taking off from work. So right here, any fool should know, Momma was especially mad.

Before Momma had boiled one pot of water for either her oatmeal or coffee; before Momma had brushed her teeth real good; taken off her bathrobe, or taken the curlers out of her hair, she had that smart son of hers all the way out of bed and was dragging him by the nape of his neck to the car.

Oh yes, any fool should know just where in a few good men they were headed. Momma had had about all she could stand. The Marines, you know, were looking all over town for a few good men, and here Momma had a good and smart one caught by the nape of his neck.

With the curlers, bathrobe, funky mouth and all, Momma dropped her son off at the recruiting station. She was going around the corner for that night's supper, but when she got back, she wanted them papers signed.

Momma pulled away from the curb shaking her head. She was so mad one of her curlers was on fire. Just who in the world did that child think he was testing? Yes he was a smart young man, but he would never know as much as his Momma. Did he not know that?

When Momma returned her bright young son was not

waiting outside as she expected him to be. Momma, however, gave the child a few more minutes.

Maybe he had a lot of papers to sign. Maybe he was already at the point of swearing in. Maybe he left the country already. Or, just maybe Momma would get home and find a letter already on the table from him, telling her all about how he was so smart he skipped right on into a General's outfit. Momma was getting more and more anxious, but she waited. Momma waited thirty minutes or more.

Enough of the waiting. Any fool should know Momma had to know.

Momma hopped out of the car and marched straight into the recruiting office. Momma rounded one corner and breezed on by a Marine and Air Force Recruiter chatting over a cup of coffee. Momma didn't bother to introduce herself. Once she found her son she figured they would know all about who she was.

Damn! There he was. There was Momma's gifted child sitting in an office slumped over in a chair looking all glum.

Any fool should know Momma wanted to know why he was slumped over in the chair and looking so glum. That wasn't any way for a tough smart young man to sit. Where was that rough and tough smart bad boyz image? That's another thing momma hated. She hated wimpy whiny boys.

"What?"

Momma almost cart-wheeled backwards when she heard what that smart child of hers had to say. He had been sitting there all that time because he didn't have a pen.

See. These were the things children didn't know that mommas did know. Momma had resources. Momma hadn't been his momma all that time without good cause.

Momma dove right over the recruiter's desk and went scrounging for a pen.

"I got cha' pen," Momma went yelling.

Momma was really hot. Now all her hair curlers were on fire. But Momma didn't care. Momma didn't even care that both recruiters had turned around and were laughing at her.

"Ma'am. Ma'am," the Air Force recruiter went, returning to his office. "You can't do that."

Sparks and flames were licking up everywhere; all around Momma and upside her gifted young son's head too. Momma was now fully engulfed in flames. Any fool should know Momma was a set on fire blazing hot mess.

Momma pulled that child of hers out of the chair promising the recruiters she was coming back. Oh yes, Momma was coming back. She was coming back with those papers signed, too.

But any fool should know Momma never went back. That gifted child of hers went straight from the recruiter's office, directly into college.

SLIP AND SLIDE SCRAP'EMS

Scrap'ems, short for Slip and Slide Scrap'ems, was the middle grandbaby. On a grand scale, in comparison to his other cousins, it might have seemed as if he got the most of his grandparent's time and attention. But let Scrap'ems break it down, he'd probably say things was about equal.

Because his Mom-Mom and Pop-Pop practically raised him, he got both the unwanted attention, and the doting grandparenty attention. That's how things equaled out. He got the type of attention his aunties and father used to get, along with the extra hugs and gifts his cousins didn't always get. Scrap'ems got the best part of both worlds, which sometimes he considered himself blessed, and then other times…

…well, there were other times when Mom-Mom, as usual, was doting a little way too much over this grandbaby. Mom-Mom heard Scrap'ems had an 8th grade dance coming up. She told everyone she could think of about the dance. She was just so proud of seeing her grandbabies grow, especially this grandchild who she had literally watched grow from diapers, all the way to attending his first 8th grade dance.

The day of Scrap'ems dance Mom-Mom got off early from work and zipped right home to see him before he left. She had a picture of him all etched out in her mind; a jazzy tie, freshly pressed white shirt, dark slacks, decent dress shoes, and his charming self to hit it all off with. But then one foot in the door and there was Scrap'ems looking like he needed a ride home to get dressed.

Mom-Mom was curious. "Are you sure it's okay to wear jeans?"

Back in her day kids got dress for things like dances. In fact, kids couldn't wait to find a reason to dress up. They would have a whole house of women up all night mending hems, and stuffing shoes, and cutting through somebody's property to borrow Uncle Joe's one white cotton shirt. Those nights used to be a party within itself. With not much else to do, folks made a big deal out even the smallest events.

But true, that was a long time ago; something like a half century ago. Eighth grade dances were hardly a big deal anymore. Here Mom-Mom had told everyone, yet only she had taken the dance to a new level of excitement.

So Mom-Mom didn't contest how Scrap'ems was dressed. She would accept the baggy jeans hanging off him, the jersey, the hoody, and the whole wrinkled nine yards if it was okay with the school.

They hopped in ole' Kerbeck and pulled up to the dance where Scrap'ems hopped out of the car and dashed straight for the door.

Mom-Mom smiled. Though Kerback wasn't the Big Blue Valley, she totally understood his reason for not wanting to sit in the car too long. Shucks, his aunties had done worse than that. They used to beg her for rides to dances and then would tell her to drop them off two blocks away. At least Scrap'ems allowed her to pull up to the front door, and when he hopped out, Kerbeck wasn't still moving.

Mom-Mom sat in Kerbeck a while, smiling at the thought. Her grandbaby was going to his first 8th grade dance.

That did it.

Mom-Mom wanted to steal a peep. Just one little itty bitty peep and then she would be satisfied. She wanted to see the grandchild who she had seen out of pampers, and off the bottle; the same grandchild who would nestle up to her late at night and allow her to kiss the top of his head until he had fallen off to sleep, enjoying his first 8th grade dance.

Mom-Mom turned off the motor and struggled out of Kerbeck. It always was a chore for Mom-Mom to get around. Though her new knees where pretty much state of the art, they still weren't her original knees, and they certainly hadn't been planted into her original body.

She hobbled on up the steps that lead to the dance, and pulled on the heavy door. A young woman stood on the other side. The young woman was taking tickets and sort of monitoring the children as they entered.

At first glance, looking around the elaborately decorated room, Mom-Mom nearly lost her breath. And it wasn't because she had huffed and puffed up a tall group of steps either. All the children, except her grandchild, were dressed—really dressed—like how children in her hay-day dressed for dances.

"Excuse me," Mom-Mom said leaning into the young woman at the door, "I thought the children were told they didn't have to dress up; that they could wear jeans."

"Oh no," the young woman exclaimed, "the only reason we let your grandchild in here dressed as he was, was because he told us his grandmother couldn't afford to buy him anything to wear."

Mom-Mom's eyes started to tear and narrow, which Mom-Mom's eyes narrowing wasn't an easy feat. Mom-Mom had to work extra hard to get her eyes to slither to slits. It was a deliberate maneuver.

How dare that boy lie. And lie on her no less. She didn't even have to plow back to remembering those unfortunate children who didn't have a big sister like Louise, who had stayed up half the night making sure she was dressed in the best for all the big dances. She stopped right at the nerve of that child blaming her for being dressed the way he was.

"Excuse me," Mom-Mom said again, only that time she said it indigently while zeroing in on Scrap'ems.

"Ronnie!"

Mom-Mom was calling Scrap'ems by his real name—long, loud, and clear. Everyone heard her, including Scrap'ems. And everyone knew what that meant. When a parent called a child by his or her real name, it meant only one thing—trouble.

"Child, you just wait until I get to you," Mom-Mom vented, wheezing her way over to Scrap'ems. It was not her intention to embarrass him, but at that point all she was thinking about was how she was going to grab a hold of his ear and twist it right out of the gym. How dare he lie on her was all she had on her mind.

Scrap'ems didn't budge, though he may have wanted to. He couldn't. And he couldn't ignore her either. Mom-Mom was too loud. He also couldn't run. He still had to go home. All Scrap'ems could do was stay put until Mom-Mom had finished plowing her way through his classmates, hustling over to him.

Mom-Mom snatched Scrap'ems up by his hoody and led him right to the door. "Come with me," she hissed.

Scrap'ems knew better than to frown. Making a scene was the furthest thought from his mind. He definitely wasn't looking forward to his Mom-Mom using the rest of her teeth and tongue and pointer finger on him. Scrap'ems didn't fool around with Mom-Mom when she was this hot. She was as sweet as bean pie on any given day, but not when she was hot.

"We'll be back," Mom-Mom hissed to the young woman as she whisked Scrap'ems out the door.

Inside Kerbeck Scrap'ems tried to explain, but Mom-Mom wasn't having it. How dare he make her look like a fool. He didn't have anything to wear, not because she couldn't buy him an outfit. It was because he hadn't asked.

And he wasn't going to sulk up on her either. She was taking him home to get properly dressed, and then she was bringing right back to the dance. And oh, he was going to have a good time, she promised him that.

Mom-Mom shook and shivered all the way over to the neighborhood mall. In one nine by twelve store she grabbed a pair of slacks, a dress shirt, a belt, and a pair of socks off one rack. She then rushed over to Mike Stevens and snatched a pair of shoes off a table.

She hustled the two bags and Scrap'ems right home where she forced him into the clothes, going as far as to even stuff his shoes.

When she was done, Scrap'ems was in tears. He begged Mom-Mom to let him stay home. He didn't like the way he looked. He could never face his friends.

He pleaded and pleaded, but to no avail. It was too late. That's what he got for lying. You don't lie on Mom-Mom. He should have asked his father.

Mom-Mom shoved Scrap'ems right back in Kerbeck

and zipped back over to the dance. Within thirty minutes it was said and done. Scrap'ems was back at the dance, where that time it was she who had to force him out of the car.

Scrap'ems pleaded once more, telling Mom-Mom the shoes were too slippery. He kept sliding, which he thought he might slip and fall.

Well Mom-Mom had an answer for that one too. She told Scrap'ems to slide his feet back and forth over the pavement to give the bottom of the shoes a good scrapen'. As an added incentive she hollered after him, "and have fun!"

Oh yes, had not Mom-Mom promised Scrap'ems he was going to have a good time?

Two Peas in a Pod

Hell yeah the crazy bat raised two brats. That's because it don't take no special skills to raise brats. All you have to do is lay on a couch in jeans you don't get out of long enough to wash, and act all silly when one of your brats does something like kick the television over.

Good grief, it wasn't like her show was on, or as if she was watching a worthwhile show like Buffy, or a scary movie even. The television broke during a commercial.

Throwing telephones and her old raggedy purses and shoes at us over accidents was totally unnecessary. I wanted to throw my shoe back at her, except I knew if I did, her silly tail might have broken my legs, and still made me walk, barefoot, to and from school.

You know that woman actually had the nerve to be praying one of us flipped out on her in a store. That's why I'm so glad we broke the TV. She watched too much television anyway. Everybody knows white kids ain't no more monsters than black kids, yet some fool telling real bad jokes—on TV of course—had her believing black kids didn't fall out in supermarkets. Like hissy fits were connected to skin color.

Well I sure showed her. I fell right out in the middle of the floor of a nice size super-sized store. Yep, I liked to have busted my head I flipped back so far. And I made sure my legs and feet were way up there in the air.

I kicked and screamed and hollered loud enough for child protective services in every county and division to come running to my aid. I wanted that whatever I wanted right then. I wasn't waiting until she finished her business. And she could be sure I wasn't waiting on if, and only if I behaved.

But then there was the crazy bat, in the middle of the floor too, dancing around me acting all happy and silly. She was up in the store talking about how she had waited all her life for that moment. Can you imagine? I'm telling you she's a zingy bat. I hope the zingy bat broke every one of her fingernails getting me up off the floor.

Zingy Lulu had no cause to be showing out like that. The zingy bat knew her brats were brats. She knew that when she heard the first words that came out of my mouth. I was still in pampers, feet couldn't even reach the floor, and I was talking up a whole can of whipass.

That's right. You should have heard my first sentence, and then seen the crazy look on the zingy bat's face. Zingy Lulu was standing there, blocking my view I might add, with one hand covering her mouth... looking all surprised!

I told the zingy bat to move the you know what out of my way—standing there looking all silly, talking about how she couldn't believe it.

Couldn't believe what?

Lulu wasn't no princess. The zingy bat had more like inherited a stone and had the audacity to try and pass it along. Walking around town thinking she was all that. You should have seen her in somebodies Safeway. Somebodies Safeway you hear? ...Acting all cute... buying a big piece of brown beef... and oh yeah... and one banana too.

Shopping with the 6pm crew because she got a halfway decent job and buying one banana don't make her cute. And that old fool ringing up our sh—, asking if we were sisters, don't make her look young either.

I wanted to spin zingy Lulu's wig around twice she made me so mad. Standing up there grinning like a cheap floozy knowing good and cheesy well she don't look nowhere near like a sister of mines. Maybe my nana, or my great grandmammy even.

That's it! When I have kids, which by the way, I'm going to make Lulu have and raise since she knows so much—but I'm going to have the brats calling her Granny Wannda.

Yep, little Sally Sue or Billy Bob will be calling crazy Lulu, Granny Wannda. And yeah, yeah, yeah... and wann, wann, wann... ain't no sense in whining about old crazy granny Wannda and how this brat of hers talks like this. Don't feel sorry for her. Like I said, crazy Granny Wannda knows every flippity flap dang thing.

Aside from throwing the purses and shoes and temper tantrums, Crazy Granny Wannda even knows how to star in her little one-woman show picking up brats like me off the floor. Granny Wannda knows how to cook, and sing, and dance, and she thinks she even knows how to patch up things.

We thought she knew how to cut hair, but after she took to the other brat's head, cutting tracks so wide in his head I can still hear the brat yelling, we knew she didn't know everything. Granny Wannda had to pack up her pinking sheers and go out and purchase a real set of sheers.

It was Sunday—Sunday night. Crazy Granny Wannda was out all night looking for clippers. Ha, ha. Serves the crazy bat right. She won't let no one mess with her hair though. No one can manicure her nails, pluck her brows, or cure her ailments either. Zingy Lulu knows how to do all of that herself. Thank goodness she still allows the dentist to clean her teeth. But one day soon, I'll bet she'll even have the tools to handle that herself.

Nobody can do anything for that woman, which does nothing but put more pressure on me. Just like that I'm down five hundred bucks trying to keep up with the zingy know-it-all bat. You don't think I'll let just anyone do my manicures and pedicures? For the sake of class, hell no!

What this means is that I now have to visit a salon that bathes and massages me, waxes me, and take care of my nails and feet. That's the only way I can keep ahead of the flooz.

I finally had to tell crazy Granny Wannda a thing or two. I had to slow the flooz down. She was just getting way out of hand. The flooz needed to be set down and told because all day long listening to her drone on and on about mess I didn't need to or want to hear was just getting on my last nerve.

When I cry, I don't need to see her jaws going. And I don't need her damn two cents either. I already know she has the answer. That's whole point about why I'm crying. I see Lulu's lips flapping, and I'm bawling. Crazy Granny Wannda's gift to gab starts really showing out, and I'm bawling even louder. I know Lulu ain't all that, and I'm falling over backwards bawling. And then I hear crazy Granny Wanda's flippin' patronizing voice, and I just pass out.

That's why it would be so nice to stuff crazy Granny in my closet. That way, when I need Lulu she'll be right where I stuffed her. And when I don't, I can close the door and same thing, which by the way, I told crazy granny Wannda this.

By then I was up to calling her a wildebeest. Crazy Granny Wannda had gone so far out she had turned into a real wildebeest. I think I was even calling her a barracuda as well. I had to. I had to tone that attitude of hers way down. Keeping up just got too hard.

I only wished I could have set the wildebeest straight a lot earlier—a lot earlier like before she turned into a barracuda. The barracuda had the unmitigated gull to one day reach up and grab me in the collar with her disjointed, double-jointed crooked fingers. That did it.

True Cuda got me my first real job. But I helped her too. Ask her how many assistants she had run off; and how many jobs she had run through to do what I did for her on try one. I wasn't even out of high school and I was directing callers, taking messages, and filing her catastrophic piles of papers like no one had done before me. And the best part was everyone in the office appreciated me.

Lulu couldn't have done all that. And she sure as a Nightmare on Elm Street couldn't have gotten that other brat of hers to do all this either.

The other brat was supposedly the smart brat, too. But all the way to the day she would have to let the brat go, she would have been dragging him out of bed. Then once she got him out of bed good, she would have been propping him up and then forcing him to iron something decent to wear.

Actually, she probably would have been picking out and ironing his clothes herself. And then once at work, she would have been fighting with him for eight hours straight, trying to get an hour's worth of work out of him.

The funny part would have been how everyone not just liked the brat, but how everyone would have been ranting and raving over him.

And the brat?

Well, the brat himself would have been strolling around the office talking about how the flooz took the job way too serious. But she really did. From the couch to corporate, Lulu took to raising her brats like an oath of office.

But, you know what? I love my flooz. That's right. I love my floozy Mamacita.

I have to give it to my Chica. Her couch may have been worn out from extensive wear and tear, and her denims faded so badly it looked like she was wearing a belt and a thong, but at the end of it all—shoes, purses, yaking and ranting and raving buck wild—she really did make the best brats. Just what in a straightening her out do you think it was that gave me this mouth?

THE BOYS

The boys came during an era when all the old school versions of rearing children were in garbage heaven. The recycling technicians had picked up the degenerative materials, squished it to mulch, delivered it to the garbage pallbearers, and on to garbage heaven it went.

Major psychology books written on rearing children were circulating. Mass numbers of these books were now at the disposal of anyone requiring the slightest bit of information on child rearing.

No longer were new mothers getting parenting advice from the perspectives of other female relatives and friends. They were getting advice from physicians, television, documentaries, books, the Internet, and new legislation too.

Children in this era were handled with extreme caution. They had significant rights, so you had to be careful with how you talked to them, touched them, and disciplined them. These children were more fragile than the generation A through Y children. Groups of courts determined concepts could be explained to children in the cyberspace era.

However, parents and guardians working from a limited understanding of cyberspace concepts, ended up having to tiptoe around these youngsters, hoping their little cyberspace splendors would remain splendors and not turn into little cyberspace monsters. This was the environment in the new millennium children operated in.

The boys, at only 5 and 6 years old, knew all about their rights when they decided to take a fishing expedition with Pop-Pop. They were backpacking a wealth of information.

They knew at certain wavelengths the sun's ultraviolet rays were harmful to their skin, and wearing safety helmets reduced injuries 99% of the time, and fish were more active during the morning or evening when there wasn't as much light coming from the sun.

The fishing trip Pop-Pop had taken to the Pocono Mountains over fifty years ago, he could go on and put in a scrapbook, and from there take directly to the cellar. This was a whole new era. Pop-Pop didn't have a thing to worry about. New technologies like weather bureaus and weather radars, CNN and the Advanced Hydrologic Prediction Service had taken over, infusing new and improved tools for the little cyberspace people to use.

Pop-Pop needn't tarry or toil. The boys had him covered. All Pop-Pop needed to concern himself with was the fact that they were going to have to get going if they wanted to catch any fish.

The boys gathered up their fishing rods and store-bought artificial bait and led Pop-Pop to the lake. See, it wouldn't have been like this back in Pop-Pop's day. First of all, there would have been no fishing rods, at least not the kind Wal-Mart sold. And there certainly wouldn't have been any artificial bait. In fact, the entire scenario would have been shifted—a whole lot.

Had Pop-Pop's grandfather taken him and his brothers fishing, they would have been instructed to grab a stick and some twine and follow along. Right from there they would have known they were going fishing, which if somehow they hadn't figured it out, they would have figured it out when they reached the fishing hole.

Children had no liberties back then. The only privilege children had, which really wasn't a privilege, but more like a right of passage, was the privilege to watch, listen, and learn.

The hike over to the lake wasn't far. One of the boys however, the oldest—Mr. D, didn't care a whole lot for a whole lot of walking. But he was curious enough though.

The science of seeing fish being lured to bait and fastening its lips over the hook was intriguing. Oh, no wait. It was interesting learning the techniques used to lure fish out of water. Those were topics children Mr. D's age sometimes shared in class. Otherwise, had it not been for the interesting aspect of fishing, Mr. D would not have been interested. In the same way Mr. D settled who put that one cookie in his hand, would have been the same way he would have settled whether or not he was taking the hike.

Mr. D's little brother, the Alligator—a nickname acquired not so much for his love of reptiles either—however was different. He enjoyed all aspects of nature. Pass him the lizards, the frogs, the turtles, and the furry creatures with the grizzly eyes. While most children the Alligator's age backed away from those creatures resembling trolls, the alligator came out of the womb fearless of creatures with the terrifying faces making creepy noises.

The Alligator wasn't yet walking when he was sticking his fingers in snakes' mouths—to check the snake's teeth. For his 5th birthday party an albino python was his guest of honor—and still yet, none of this had anything to do with the meaning behind his nickname.

Pop-Pop and the boys hiked towards a lake where they came upon a path that split in different directions. The choices were simple. They could either walk along the grassy embankment towards the bridge, or follow the trail leading below the bridge, directly to the lake.

Pop-Pop wanted to walk along the grassy embankment. He knew the trail leading to the lake would be littered with all sorts of insectivores that wouldn't take kindly to being disturbed. The very moment they started walking over the rocks, the critters were going skip, hop, pop up, and attack whoever dared to disturb their peace. This was one of the lessons the rites of passage had taught him.

Mr. D and the Alligator however, weren't outfitted with this data. The boy's were backpacking a more advanced degree of technological logic. They were sharp and their information was a whole lot more current than Pop-Pop's. They had already estimated the proximity of the bridge to the lake, versus the trail that banked around the edge of the lake.

In today's cycle of innovation they knew it was all about convenience and speed. It made perfect sense to cast their lines directly into the lake, as opposed to hurling lines over a bridge. The likelihood of catching a fish or two would be that much quicker and easier the closer they were to the water.

Navigating the trail however, wasn't easy. As Pop-Pop surmised, the very moment they stepped foot on the rocks the critters awoke. This complicated matters. It complicated matters because the trail was hillier than Pop-Pop first assessed. Avoiding an insect with a testy temperament, while keeping their balance, was going to be tricky.

Pop-Pop kept vigilant, his degree of concern increasing with each step. One of the boys could have fallen, namely Mr. D who was trailing behind. Pop-Pop also was concerned for himself. He wasn't a spring chicken anymore. One slip for him could have easily amounted to a whole lot more than a bruised elbow or a skinned knee. A little spit would hardly heal the injury Pop-Pop could have caused himself. Pop-Pop could have messed around and slipped his way up on a gurney.

Pop-Pop encouraged the boys to watch their step as they finagled their way down the hilly trail. They had almost made it to the bottom of the trail when Mr. D suddenly began screaming and hollering. Pop-Pop immediately stopped and turned around.

Mr. D was hollering and screaming something fierce. One of the annoyed insects—Mr. D screamed something about it being a bee—had woke up and started fussing. Mr. D fussed back, fanning and slapping, and screaming and yelling. The bee, however, looked like it was winning.

Pop-Pop yelled for Mr. D to calm down, but at the time calm down wasn't making much sense to Mr. D. After several more swings, Mr. D decided enough was enough. Mr. D no longer was in a mood for fishing, and he certainly wasn't about to calm down.

Mr. D took off. Rocks, slopes, and all the way up the hilly terrain, Mr. D got the heck out of there. Pop-Pop couldn't do a thing except desperately follow the direction in which he had taken off.

Partially frozen, and partially wavering on rocks as if he was surfing on a high-beam, Pop-Pop followed Mr. D up the hill and out of sight. That's when Pop-Pop noticed they weren't alone. There were men working on the bridge in the direction in which Mr. D had taken off. This caused Pop-Pop even more concern. Now his grandchild was headed in a direction that could possibly become an Amber Alert.

Pop-Pop would never forgive himself if something awful happened. There would be no account convincing enough to revive the Black Table and restore it to its original condition if something bad happened to the boys on his watch.

Just when Pop-Pop started to turn around and suggest to the Alligator they had better wrap up the fishing expedition, something suddenly caught him from the back by his shirt. Pop-Pop wasn't sure what it was. He twisted one way, but was stopped midway. He twisted the opposite way, and again was stopped midway. After a few more twists and turns, and one brief reach around to the center of his back, Pop-Pop realized what had snared him in the awkward position.

The Alligator eager to cast his line and reel in a fish had hooked onto the biggest catch on the lake—Pop-Pop.

ACKNOWLEDGEMENTS

Preoccupied with whether I was keeping my word about uplifting spirits in need of uplifting, I got to wondering if I needed to scrap the opening, or the entire book altogether.

Being as honest as I could throughout the Black Table, I thought maybe I was a little too honest. There wasn't enough sugarcoating going on, and too much, albeit humorous, but ignominious focus in the way I presented the stories. I kept hoping by the time I reached the end, the love and appropriate importance of our stories would show up.

I thank God, it did.

Next to God, I also thank my father.

Dad, thank you for providing the platform and tools that although I, at this late great date was having difficulty properly interpreting, I now appreciate for seeing how it has not only kept us together as a family, but has facilitated making us better communicators. Being frank and direct, and sometimes stubborn but usually silly, while incorporating a concern for each other's views and feelings are integral communicating factors so very vital to pass on. And thanks too, for adding the *flavor*!

God truly has blessed our table.